House Doctor

House Doctor

Ann Maurice
with Fanny Blake

HarperCollins*Publishers*

First published in Great Britain in 2000 by HarperCollins

an imprint of HarperCollins*Publishers*
77–85 Fulham Palace Road
London W6 8JB

www.**fire**and**water**.com

Design: Neal Townsend for Essential Books
Picture research: Emma Dickens for Essential Books

The right of Ann Maurice to be identified as the author of this work has been asserted by her in accordance with the Copyright, Designs and Patents Act 1988

7 9 10 8

Printed and bound in Great Britain by Bath Press Colourbooks

A catalogue record for this book is available from the British Library

ISBN 0–00–220210–7

acknowledgments

My thanks go to the following people: Mary Cummings, my dear friend and mentor who has been an inspiration in every way; Jocasta Innes, who is responsible for my being here in the UK; Daisy Goodwin for recognizing my potential and making *House Doctor* a success; Basi Akpabio for doing the impossible, and making it work; Ed Stobart for constantly presenting me with challenges; all the directors— Richard Farmbrough, Joanna Bartholomew, Anna Ratsey, Helen Simpson—the researchers, production crew, especially our cameraman, Paul Curran, and soundman, Sebastian, for making such fantastic programmes; my makeover staff who made miracles happen, and especially my assistant, Darren Ayers, whose talent and commitment were my constant support through the many highs and lows; Channel 5; all the contributors who allowed us to wreak havoc in their homes and lives in order to make a programme.

I'd especially like to thank my co-author Fanny Blake, all at Essential Books, Cat Ledger and Emma Cockshutt at Talkback, and Polly Powell and Fiona Screen at HarperCollins.

Finally, my thanks go to my partner, Tim, my daughters, Lauryn and Melanie and my dog, Floyd, who have had to live without me, but who still love me.

House Doctor is a **TalkBack** *production*

Contents

setting the stage for SUCCESS

Congratulations! You have made the big decision to sell your home. Well, whether you are just about to phone your estate agent to begin the process or have been trying for some time unsuccessfully to get that sale, I encourage you to read this book. By following my simple, commonsense tips you will be able to get the highest and best price for your home and get it fast.

What is this mysterious secret that I bring with me from across the Pond? It is called "Home Staging", and has become hugely successful in my home state of California. If this concept is an unfamiliar one to most of you, let me explain. Simply put, home staging is a marketing technique. (And most of you will agree that we Americans are masters at the art of marketing.) It is a manner of presenting a home for sale so that it will appeal to the broadest buying audience, "setting the stage" as it were, so that when the ready, willing and able buyer walks through the door, they are immediately hooked. There is nothing here that is dishonest in any way, and no trickery is involved. It is a simple technique that makes the most of what your home already has, thus allowing prospective buyers to see it in its most favourable light and — more importantly — to see themselves living there. Home staging enables a buyer to mentally "move in" to your home.

This technique is not purely theoretical on my part: rather, it comes from years of direct experience. Prior to managing my current successful interior design business in San Francisco, Touché Designs, I devoted thirteen years to a career as an estate agent, selling homes in what was historically one of the most competitive property markets ever. Within a short time it became increasingly clear to me what it was that made certain houses sell rapidly for a maximum price and what caused others to sit on the market for weeks, even months, without even a glimmer of interest. Assuming a house was fairly priced, well located, had no apparent structural problems and was in the hands of a competent estate agent, it came down to one thing, and one thing only: presentation.

When I decided to leave the property business and study interior design, the move from being a house seller to a house stager was a natural one. Because of my personal connections from my years as an estate agent (as well as my increasing knowledge and ability in interior design) it didn't take long for my new career to take off. I began to be called in by other estate agents as well as their clients to prepare their homes for the market. After all, from both the agents' and the sellers' perspectives, what could be better than a quick sale at a premium price? The results were amazing. The homes that I staged were selling within the first few weeks (sometimes days) after coming on the market, for near to and sometimes even more than the asking price. With results like these, the benefits of home staging became obvious throughout the industry.

OK, you say, so this idea works in California, but will it be as successful in England? Why not, I ask? In a country where two thirds of the population own their own homes (well above the European average), which for most people are their most valuable asset, wouldn't the same principles apply? Judging by my experiences while working on *House Doctor* I would have to say emphatically, yes.

Great Britain is currently experiencing one of the greatest property booms ever, yet the homes that were chosen for "house doctoring" on the television series were just not selling. There were various reasons why, and each home presented a different challenge for the *House Doctor* team. Several had owners who had lost faith that their homes would ever sell and a few of them actually doubted that home staging could make a difference. Yet the end result was that all of the homes in the series were sold after having been properly staged.

Why hadn't these houses sold on their own? The sellers all wanted a sale of their homes so that they could get on with their lives. They all thought that they had done what was necessary — a bit of straightening, perhaps some decorating, maybe a few new plants for the garden. They thought that they could sit back and relax until an offer came in. However, all were stuck, waiting. What could all these sellers possibly have been doing wrong?

I am often asked to define the most common mistake sellers make when trying to sell their homes. The answer is fairly simple: they assume that, because they are comfortable in their own home and love it just the way it is, a prospective buyer will feel the same. Nothing could be further from the truth. Buyers need to be able to visualise themselves and their things in a home before even thinking of making an offer. They have to be able to see it as theirs, not yours. Which is not something that takes place purely by chance.

It is a proven fact that buyers are willing to pay a higher price for a home that they feel they do not have to put a lot of time and money into putting right. But they are not often able to see through your "personality" to the home of their dreams. It is amazing how blind you can become to the things you live with day to day. Small things that you have grown accustomed to, like your untidy garden, unfinished repairs, unnecessary clutter, dingy carpet or even your dog could be costing you money, or perhaps, more importantly, losing you that long-awaited sale.

I am not referring to some mysterious secret here. This is not rocket science, there's no complicated technique; rather, it is purely an issue of common sense. The key is to "neutralise" your home — in effect, to take your personality out of the house so that buyers can imagine themselves as the one living there. You need to detach yourself from your home in order to be able to move on and achieve your dream. You are no longer living in your home, you are selling it, and these are two very different things. I realise that these may sound like harsh words, but if this concept seems strange to you at first, perhaps uncomfortable or even unnatural, it is nonetheless true. Remember, though, that this is only temporary. It is a means to an end. You do want to move, don't you?

So, then, how do you start? The first and most difficult thing to do is to take a good look at your home critically and objectively through "buyer's eyes". How would a complete stranger who is interested in buying a house in your neighbourhood view your home? Remember, there is always the competition. Keeping this thought foremost in your mind, begin by standing across the street and imagine you are a prospective buyer driving by. Would you be interested in stopping to view your home? Does it compare well to the other houses on the street? Does its exterior make you want to go inside and see more? If not, then make a careful note of any possible improvements which would make your home more inviting. Kerb appeal is critical — after all, if the buyer doesn't make it to the front door, you will have lost him or her. There are no second chances.

Next, go inside. Pen and paper in hand, go carefully through each room noting anything that needs clearing, cleaning, mending or brightening. The most important rooms are the living room, main bedroom, kitchen and bathroom, so concentrate your efforts here if you have to choose. Be very tough on yourself. Remember you are seeing your home through a buyer's eyes. Buyers are very critical and they tend to focus on anything that might give them an excuse to make you a lower offer. Why give them the opportunity? Anything that could raise a possible objection in a buyer's eyes should be taken care of beforehand. This effort will mean money in the bank for you. Don't forget your garden and any other outside space — including storage and parking areas. These are often neglected by home sellers and can sometimes make the difference between getting and losing a sale. Always bear in mind that buyers need to feel they are getting the most for their money.

Now that you have completed your list, go back through your house and make sure that you have left nothing out. If there is any question in your mind as to whether or not something should be done, do it. Trust me on this one. It will be worth it in the long run. Remember — no pain, no gain.

Now you have the formula for success. The rest is up to you. My experience shows that if you use this technique to prepare your home for sale, your expenditure of time, money, and effort will not go unrewarded. Your house will sell quickly and for its highest and best price.

I am thrilled to have been able to introduce this concept of "home staging" to British home owners via *House Doctor*. My greatest satisfaction of all, though, is in being able to help so many people move on and realise their dreams.

Ann Maurice
December 1999

"First impressions are often what make or break a sale"

Chapter One
EXTERIORS

When selling your house, don't ever underestimate the importance of how it looks from the outside. First impressions are often what make or break a sale. It's not much use having a perfect designer-style interior if the outside of the building is so scruffy that prospective buyers drive right past.

Begin by standing across the road from your house and take a good long look. Can you put your hand on your heart and say that its appearance can't be improved? If there's a broken-down car quietly rusting outside, get it moved. Is there anything that needs painting? Is it perfectly clear where your property begins and the neighbours' ends? It's important that the boundaries are clear—a buyer wants to know exactly what he or she is looking at. To this end, you may want to invest in some fencing, a brick wall or hedging plants.

Is your front garden just a bit neglected compared to the horticultural wonder at the back of the house? Mow the lawn, tidy the edges and invest in some attractive bedding plants to pretty it up, or at least tidy up the plants that are there. If it's autumn, sweep up the dead leaves. Clear it of the children's tricycles and get rid of those old dog's bones. This is a house we're trying to sell, not a cemetery. Improve the approach to the front door, perhaps by lining the front steps or a short path with a few potted plants, which will lead a visitor in. If you have trees in the front garden, ask yourself whether they need pruning. You don't want the trees to block the view of the house and, most importantly, they shouldn't block the light coming into the house.

What about the paintwork on the house? Is it in reasonably good repair? It may be worth having it redone. Replace any dead plants in window boxes so that you have a welcoming display instead. Mend any broken guttering or slipped roof slates.

Clean windows make a huge difference to the appearance of a house. Clear all window sills as they look messy from the street, and make sure all curtains and blinds are evenly drawn and hanging properly.

Even if you don't need to redecorate the outside of the house, think about painting or revarnishing your front door. It can give a surprising lift to the general appearance. Polish the letterbox, knocker and the handle. If the bell doesn't work, take off the note saying so and mend it. Then buy a new front door mat, preferably one that says "Welcome". It is a terrific subliminal message.

When you've thoroughly checked the exterior and done everything you can to ensure that it clearly says the property has been loved and cared for, THEN it's time to think about inside. Remember, a buyer usually makes a decision to buy within the first thirty seconds of entering a home, so make sure that a potential buyer enters your house in a positive frame of mind.

DIAGNOSIS
& cures

Nobody in their right mind would have wanted to get further than the front door of this house. The whole façade urgently needed major first aid. The building work had been left incomplete, with ugly piles of rubble heaped up outside. The front door was dull and uninviting. If the owners had taken so little trouble outside, what on earth would the interior be like? A clue was given by the filthy old curtains at the front window, while the lack of curtains elsewhere made the house look unloved and empty. The paintwork was in terrible condition, both on the frames and the stonework. The car parking area was unfinished and made the path to the front door muddy and unattractive.

clean up

The first thing to do was get rid of the general mess that had accumulated outside. Once that had been done, we concentrated on cleaning up the mess that might once have been the front garden. We decided to separate the path from the parking area with a low wall. We then painted the front door and gave the letterbox and handle a thorough polish. We finished off the windows by treating the woodwork with primer/undercoat and then painting it a brilliant white. However, it was as important to clear up the inside of the house as the outside. We gave the windows a long overdue clean, both inside and out. Then those dreadful curtains had to go. In their place, we hung new curtains, both upstairs and downstairs. Without an enormous amount of effort or expense, the house at last looked desirable.

define

It's as important to define the external areas of the house as it is the interior ones. In this case, it was necessary to separate the parking space from the front path. The low brick wall built from stock that matched the house didn't detract from the general appearance of the house, but made a definite statement, emphasising the way to the front door. The trellised climber by the side of the door added an attractive finishing touch.

paint it

What a difference a few coats of paint make. We chose white paint for the windows so that the house would sit easily beside its neighbour. It only took a fresh coat of paint to spruce up the front door, too, making it the focal point of the exterior. This simple tactic took years off the house's appearance, making it look fresh and inviting.

the CURE

brighten

The unpainted rendering and peeling front door didn't do much for this house's kerb appeal. Whitewashing the rendering and painting the front door a new glossy colour gave the house a lift and made it stand out from its surroundings.

dress up

Clean curtains at the windows make a world of difference to the appearance of a house. Hanging them at the upstairs windows tied together the look of the exterior. Three-quarter length curtains at the downstairs window helped to maintain privacy while admitting natural light.

clean

Never forget how important it is that the windows be impeccably clean. There's nothing more depressing than staring through layers of grime, but sparkling panes give an immediate impression that a house is well cared for.

garden

The plants needed a good sorting out. After all, this was meant to be the front garden of a town house, not a nature reserve. More careful planting and some judicious pruning made the whole thing look much more managed. The impression of care and time spent will influence a buyer's perception of the inside of the house, too.

before

"The hall is the space that sets the mood for the rest of the house"

Chapter Two
ENTRANCES

Stepping from the street into the entrance hall will create a lasting impression on your potential buyer. Remember, the hall is the space that sets the mood for the rest of the house.

First of all, remove any clutter. Having done that, look at the walls. A strongly patterned wallpaper or a bold colour tends to be overpowering and can make the space seem claustrophobic. Repaint in a light, neutral shade which will effortlessly give way to the rooms that lead off it. Break up the space by hanging some pictures. A mirror will always increase the sense of space and makes for good feng shui, too.

Next, look at the floor. It's one of the areas that has the most wear and may well be showing it. If your hall is small, then consider buying a length of new carpet. If that's impractical or too costly, a judiciously placed rug will make all the difference.

Lighting is important. There's nothing worse than arriving somewhere that seems dingy and uncared for. Obviously you're not going to be able to create a new window, but you can clean the one that is already there, maximising the available light. Otherwise, look at the electrics. Would the atmosphere benefit from the addition of a new lightshade that's in keeping with the period of the house? Might it be worthwhile replacing that central spot with a simple tracking system which will throw light on the walls,

again creating the illusion of space and taking the attention towards the rooms on either side? Most important of all, replace any dud bulbs with others of the right wattage.

If you have a hall that's no more than a narrow corridor, create a focal point by using a vase of flowers on a small table, or by spotlighting a picture. If you have a particularly ugly or intrusive radiator, box it in and create a useful shelf. Similarly, you might move a burglar alarm to a more subtle place – no point in making your buyer unduly nervous.

The staircase from *Psycho* is not much of an invitation, so make sure there's a welcoming light at the top. If the stairs are narrow and steep, create a different illusion by lightening the wall colour and replacing the carpet with a paler shade. If the treads are in good condition, it may be more effective to use a runner rather than a fitted carpet. Replace and paint any missing banisters. It makes a world of difference. If you've got a slatted, banister-free staircase, then it's vital to create the illusion of something more secure. It's quite easy and inexpensive to create a banister up one side, if not both.

Again, consider breaking up that expanse of wall space with some pictures, but go easy, it's not an art gallery – too many and it will feel crowded. Personal photos can be distracting.

Now that you've ensured that the entrance to your house is a warm and inviting place, it's time to look at the rooms themselves.

DIAGNOSIS
& cures

This hall, with its stark yellow and blue colour scheme, reminded me of nothing more than a doctor's waiting room. The effect was cold and impersonal and depressingly dark. The apartment was in a to-die-for location and had sensational views, but the moment you stepped inside, all that was forgotten. The owners' choice of colours was off-puttingly dated and they had put no real thought into making their hall an inviting transition point between the outside world and where they lived. I had to inject some life into the place and convince any potential buyers that they were buying into the lifestyle evoked by the fun marina development outside. I wanted to create the illusion of width, taking the eye away from the lights and the ceiling, focusing on the walls and doors. I determined to transform it into an elegant and personable space.

colour

The first job was to repaint the length of the hall. The combination of yellow and blue was far from warm and welcoming and much too overbearing for most people's taste. Instead, we chose a honey-tinted neutral for the walls which immediately opened up the space. The blue coving, skirtings and door frames were transformed by being painted with a white gloss. And with a huge sigh of relief we said goodbye to the yellow gloss doors which also succumbed to the power of the paintbrush. We left the yellow shades and used brown, beige and gold as accent colours.

perspective

Dark and powerful colours tend to impose themselves on a space, making it smaller, whereas paler shades tend to make the walls recede. In a long, tall corridor, it was essential to try to maximise the space available, at the same time inviting the eye towards the end. The mirror adds dimension while the rug and pictures draw the eye along the hall, taking the viewer into the heart of the apartment.

personality

I'm always telling people to clear up their clutter but that doesn't mean that rooms, including halls, should be left completely bare. Staging your house is about treading a fine line between lived-in and empty. Any potential buyer wants to feel in touch with the personality of the place. This hall was completely devoid of one. Three attractive prints and a mirror soon began to talk. Finally the long expanse of floor was broken up by a toning rug.

obstacles

Although the hall is traditionally where everyone dumps stuff when they come into a home, there's no reason why your buyers should have to go through some hideous obstacle race when they try to forge a path into your home. All they'll remember is how squashed it felt. True, it wasn't bad here, but the coats still had to vanish.

FIREPLACES & RADIATORS
prescription

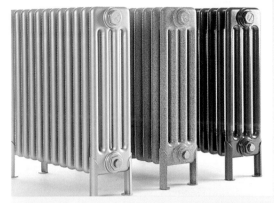

A fireplace can definitely add value to your home. It always provides an interesting focal point to a room, as well as being a practical heating source. Any existing fireplace should be properly cleaned and you should make sure that it's not being blocked from view by any furniture. If the surround doesn't fit the period of the house, visit an architectural salvage yard where you may be able to pick up something suitable at a reasonable price. If the fireplace has been boxed in, it's often worthwhile restoring it to its former glory. The same goes for that empty hole left when one has been removed. You could complete the look by investing in a fireguard and fire dogs. Light the fire if it's appropriate. Remove all the invitations and general junk from the mantelpiece where there is room for a well-chosen ornament or two — at most! Complete the look by hanging a large mirror or painting above.

Make sure that the radiators are working and the house is warm in the winter. Don't block them with furniture or curtains. Contemporary radiators and reclaimed industrial radiators can make a strong design statement, but unless you've deliberately bought your radiators with that in mind you will probably have standard functional wall fittings which add nothing to a room. However, you can change that. Boxing them in is a very simple job. If the paintwork is chipped or you want to make more or less of a feature of them, there is a wide range of specialist radiator paints available.

- **Use the finest grade wet and dry paper to take surface discolouration off a marble surround. Wet the paper and use very carefully.**
- **A decent brand of instant coffee mixed with a little water will stain a wood surround or match paler patches.**
- **Rake out the grouting between tiles and regrout before washing the tiles with soapy water.**
- **Black grout is a good idea for fireplace tiles — smoke won't stain it. Alternatively, stain the existing grout black.**
- **Repolish all cast-iron work with graphite paste.**
- **Put up a shelf over your radiator to stop the walls above getting dirty.**

SELL IT!

Elbow grease can add more value to your house than almost anything else. I can't over-emphasise how important it is to clean, clean and clean some more when you're selling your house. The kitchen and the bathroom are the two most important rooms to get absolutely spotless, but it shouldn't stop there. Dust every surface, ornament and lampshade that you possess. Make sure that the ashes are removed from the fireplace and that a fire is newly laid. The fire surround, whether tiles, slate or marble, should be positively gleaming.

SOURCES

Marble Hill Fireplaces

70–72 Richmond Road
Twickenham
Middx TW1 3BE
Tel: 020 8892 1488
Fax: 020 8891 6591
Website: www.marblehill.co.uk

Bisque

London Showroom
244 Belsize Road
London NW6 8TU
Tel: 020 7586 9749
Nationwide tel: 01225 469 244
Nationwide fax: 01225 444 708

Caradon Plumbing Ltd

Lawton Road
Alsager
Stoke-on-Trent ST7 2DF
Tel: 0870 840100
Fax: 0870 840060

Classic Radiator Cover Co

Unit 2 and 5 Mountain Ash
Industrial Estate
Mountain Ash
mid Glamorgan CF45 4EY
For brochure, tel: 01443 477824

Clockwise, left to right: Instead of the trouble and expense of restoring an old fireplace, a feature can still be made using a fire surround ★ A blazing fire never fails to give heart to a home ★ Radiator paints can be used to give a new lease of life to an old radiator. Alternatively, there are modern, coloured replacements ★ A fireplace is the perfect centrepiece to a room, with a mantelpiece to display favourite ornaments ★ **Far left:** Traditional styles of radiator can be used as a feature in themselves — there's no need to box them in.

the CURE

sweep

Don't allow the front garden to let down the appearance of your house. Give the impression of a place that's regularly looked after by sweeping it properly and trimming any straggly plants.

exterior walls

The tired and stained pebble dash was smartened up with a new coat of weather-resistant paint. Any shabby bits of window frame were tidied up and given a lick of paint, too.

entry

The front door was in perfectly good condition, but looked bland and boring. Signalling the way in to your home is important and making the front door stand out is one way to do it. Painting it a striking bright blue immediately added interest to the front of the house. It also made it stand out from the crowd

disguise

Walking straight in from the street to a shabby carpet leading up the stairs is a turn-off. This entrance was smartened up by adding a runner that made any potential buyer curious to go upstairs. Plus, of course, the owners could take it with them when they moved!

before

the CURE

light

The lighter the hall is, the better, but rather than displaying kitchen appliances in all their glory, it's preferable to put up a fine curtain. This cast a veil over what was behind it but still let in some valuable light.

going up

A varnished wood banister looks better if it is in a light environment. In this typically dark Victorian entrance it helped to paint the wood with white gloss which immediately brightened the space and reflected all the available light. It also led the eye up the stairs.

storage

Is yours one of those houses which accumulates clutter on the stairs as it waits to be taken up or down? If you really can't get it together to climb those stairs in the interest of selling your house, then invest in a few stylish baskets which will at least hide the worst of the mess. And make sure that it's all gone by the time viewers come round!

table talk

The owners' dark wood table added to the generally heavy, dated and drab feeling. It wasn't expensive to replace it with a modern chrome trestle table in a style that bridged the gap between traditional and modern. Big enough to take the phone and mail, its surface also reflected the light – which was another plus in this hallway.

before

"Get rid of the junk — old magazines, bags of knitting, children's toys"

Chapter Three
RECEPTION ROOMS

Formal drawing rooms are a thing of the past, but that doesn't give you licence to present your living room as a pigsty, particularly when selling your house. Get rid of the junk — old magazines, bags of knitting, children's toys — everything must go. Remove all evidence of your pets and any lingering smells.

Weed out crowded bookshelves. The same goes for that CD collection and the videos, too. If shelves, like rooms, look crowded, it gives the impression that there isn't enough storage space. Ornaments can be used to break up shelf space, making it look bigger. If you have an empty alcove, put up some cheap shelving to provide you with both storage and display space.

If you've made a bold statement through your choice of wallpaper or paint, it makes sense to redecorate in a neutral colour. Similarly, if the carpet is overwhelming or in terrible condition, consider replacing it or sanding and varnishing the floor, using a few accent rugs to add warmth.

Comfortable sofas that are showing their age can be given an inexpensive new lease of life with a smart throw, a slipcover, or just the addition of a few suitably coloured cushions. If you've got french windows or a good fireplace, make sure they are easy to see and get to. If a sofa dominates the room, leaving little space for anything else, it may be worth replacing it with a smaller model to give a greater feeling of spaciousness.

Create a focal point. This is important in every room of the house, but especially in the sitting room, which is the one we want to feel most proud about. The focus will probably be the fireplace or whatever you choose to hang over it, so make sure this area makes a statement that complements the style of the house.

If you have a separate room which functions purely as a dining room, then ensure it looks as friendly and inviting as the rest of the house. Dining rooms can often seem rather characterless since they're comparatively rarely used. As with every other room, it's essential to clear out any clutter and to clean it thoroughly. If your table has seen better days, cover it with an attractive cloth. Nobody's going to look at what's underneath. If the walls look empty, hang a mirror (good feng shui) or some pictures.

When selling your house it is important to define the separate areas clearly, so that the buyer can easily envisage how it will work when they move in. If you don't have a dining room, there should at least be the illusion of a separate dining area, even if you only use that bit of floorspace for your husband's Scalextric! Buyers will think they are getting more for their money. Unlike you, they're not interested in the creative side of your children, so lose any artwork and homework and make it clear that this is an eating area. If you have chairs crammed round the table, remove a couple to give the impression of space and comfort. Most of all, clear away the remains of the last meal, including the ketchup bottle, salt and pepper. Nothing looks worse.

colour

The different-coloured walls vied for attention and overpowered the room, making it feel claustrophobic. They also distracted the eye from the focus of the room, the fireplace. We unified the look by repainting the walls a strong but neutral colour and re-covering the sofas in a subtle cream brocade, using brightly coloured cushions as the only accent in the room. Net hand-painted with fleurs-de-lys replaced the curtain, echoing the gothic feel of the room and allowing the shape of the window to be clearly seen.

DIAGNOSIS
& cures

This wonderfully proportioned room had a number of features that were not being made the most of. The curtain pole cut across the Victorian gothic window and the single curtain gave a sense of imbalance. The floor was covered with a dull carpet, while the multi-coloured walls and furnishings were hardly conducive to relaxing. The fireplace should have been the focal point, but it was blocked by the television and attention was distracted by the untidy bookcase.

bookcase

The contents needed to be cut to the barest essentials. The books beside the bookcase were removed, while those on it were thinned out. The filing boxes and photos also went. The cleared shelves lent a new sense of space to the room and were decorated with a well-chosen vase or two.

fireplace

The old mirror was replaced by one with a more interesting frame. Hung properly, it became a feature and made room on the mantelpiece for some decorative objects. Candles in the grate looked as effective as a fire when lit. The television was hidden and the light was moved to a better position. The vase and spiky plant complemented the room without obscuring the now strong focal point.

floor

The carpet came up to reveal a concrete floor which, with special paint effects, was made to resemble an old flagged floor. A large sisal mat which toned in with the new colour scheme took over the centre of the room to warm everything up.

table and chairs

It was important to make people want to sit at this table. So, off with the tablecloth and on with a rich but neutral-coloured runner which immediately showed it off at its best. Putting a decoration in its centre gave the whole thing focus. The old seat covers were drab and had obviously seen better days. Loose seats like this can easily be re-covered quite cheaply. Just lift them out, remove the existing covering and tack the new fabric in place before replacing them. Hey presto — a new dining-room suite.

DIAGNOSIS
& cures

Who'd want to eat in here? Everything about the room said it wasn't regularly used. The crumpled tablecloth and chairs that didn't match gave an immediately cheerless impression. As for the empty candle holders ... Everything about this room made you want to pass swiftly through it into the conservatory beyond. It was my job to make sure visitors didn't just use it as a passage but saw it as a room in its own right, a room where they might sit and enjoy themselves.

walls

The striped wallpaper was in perfectly good condition and didn't intrude. However, I did question the choice of pictures. Framed posters aren't suitable for the formality of a dining room. They're too reminiscent of student days. Instead, a framed print was hung on one wall while the other was left bare. A single picture would be lost on its own in such a space and, with one on the opposite wall, would emphasise the sense of the room as a passage. Instead, an iron screen was found with toning fabric panels. Apart from breaking up the space, it lent a softness that wasn't there before.

the outlook

Candles had to be found for the stands on either side of the french windows. Their presence immediately changed the atmosphere in the room and also helped frame the doorway which leads out into the conservatory. Or was it a laundry room? Removing all that washing was a must. Apart from not being inviting, it gave the impression that there wasn't enough space in the rest of the house for it. Even if that's the case, it's not the message you want to give your prospective buyer. A conservatory can be a big selling point, so make sure it looks at its best with some attractive furniture and plants. What could be nicer than retiring in there after you've had a delicious meal, to sit in comfort with candlelight playing on the windows. (Don't forget to clean them first!)

prescription
AMBIENCE

Staging your house is first and foremost a marketing exercise. You have to make your home seem the most desirable property in the area. Your potential buyers must leave feeling certain that this is the only house for them. Of course presenting them with an attractive home that looks as if it can be moved into without any work being done to it is essential. But there are various subliminal suggestions that you can offer which will make the place seem even more attractive. The game is to play with your buyers' senses so that you hook them into feeling comfortable. Imagine how you can make a subtle appeal to each of the five senses: sight; hearing; taste; smell; touch. Each room should be looking its best – clean, tidy, but lived in. If it's the evening, remember to turn the lights on so rooms are at their most inviting. Arrange the lights to emphasise the best features. A decoratively laid table can offer a subliminal invitation to anyone who enters. Soft music could be playing in the background. Flowers and plants help clear the air and give a feeling of life. Most effective of all can be the addition of pleasant smells. After all, no one enjoys the smell of yesterday's cooking, damp washing, cigarette smoke or pets. Your buyer will only remember the general welcoming atmosphere of the house, not the individual tricks you have used to seduce them.

Eliminate any unpleasant smells by opening windows.
Scented candles, a drop or two of vanilla essence on a light bulb or a stick of cinnamon in a warm oven smell delicious.
Pot-pourri in the living room and a bowl of lemons in the dining room or kitchen look attractive and counter any odours.
The smells of baking bread and freshly brewed coffee are notoriously seductive when it comes to showing off your home.
Play soft music but nothing that jars.
Healthy green-leaved plants refresh and contribute a sense of well-being.
Fresh flowers add colour and fragrance to a room.

SELL IT!

Be ruthless when it comes to dealing with your pets. It's easy to get used to their smell – so ask a friend to be brutally honest with you. Does your house smell? Your buyer won't want evidence of your child's pet hamsters or beloved cats and dog the moment they cross the threshold. All pets should be banished to the garage or a willing friend's while you are showing people round. Once you've got rid of any unwanted smells, tackle the problem of pet hairs. Brush and vacuum until you're sure they have all gone. Now your house is ready to show at its best.

Far left: Candles can be used to create instant atmosphere — they are soft, romantic and flattering.

★Above: Getting your home ready to be viewed needs careful thought. Open the windows wide to let the fresh air in. Make sure that all of your plants are well watered and healthy. Check that any half-burned candles are replaced with new ones. Replace any dead light bulbs, ensuring that they are the right wattage. The smell of coffee, even if from only one cup, can be enough to begin to seduce even the most hard-nosed buyer. Brightly coloured scatter cushions can be an eye-catching addition to any room, both brightening it up and giving the impression of relaxed comfort.

SOURCES

Aero
96 Westbourne Road
London W2 5RT
Tel: 020 7221 1950

Ikea Ltd
2 Drury Way
North Circular Road
London NW10 0JO
Tel: 020 8208 5600
Website: www.ikea.com

Laura Ashley
Home Customer Services
PO Box 19
Newtown
Powys SY16 1DZ
Tel: 0990 622116

Ocean Home Shopping
Freepost Lon 811
London SW8 4BR
Tel: 0800 132985

The Pier
200 Tottenham Court Rd
London
W1P 0AD
Tel: 020 7637 7001

DIAGNOSIS
& cures

The owner had clearly lost all interest here. But why ever would anyone else want to move to a place with as little soul as this? The room had no warmth and gave no subliminal invitation to sit down and relax. There was nowhere near enough furniture and the walls needed a good clean. It was essential to make this room look as if it were lived in.

ambience

Ambience was what this room lacked. The room began to come to life with the injection of colour from the rug and cushions. But using plants, pot-pourri, scented candles and the odd ornament gave it more of a chance of appealing to all the viewers' senses, making them relax and feel at home.

clutter

The only sign of life was the clutter. Those videos racked on the floor had got to go, as did the lonely-looking ornaments. The stereo system and its spaghetti of wires dominated one corner of the room. It was better placed more discreetly.

plants

There's no doubt that plants can make an enormous difference to a room. Plants in good condition, not ones that are struggling for survival, add a feeling of life and give the impression that this is a room which the owner cares for. Pots should colour-coordinate with the room.

mirror

I am very keen on using mirrors whenever possible. They create the impression of extra space and light. Their frames can be as simple or as decorative as you choose, depending on the style of your room. The other plus of buying them, of course, is that you can take them to your new home. This mirror broke up the expanse of wall and helped to make the fireplace the focal point of the room, as it should have been.

furniture

If necessary, beg, borrow or rent furniture until you move. This room was in real trouble until we borrowed the cupboard and occasional table. The natural tones of wood contrast effectively with the brick fireplace and balance the room superbly.

COLOUR SCHEMES

Colour is a very personal thing. Everybody brings their own associations to different shades, which is exactly why you shouldn't impose your taste on any potential buyer. A bright blue might remind you of your Australian holiday, but others may find it cold and uncheering. If you have a strong colour scheme in a room, try to tone the wall colour down so that it harmonises and becomes less obtrusive. This generally tends to make the room look bigger, too. Try the new colour out in at least three areas of the room so you can see how it looks in changing lights. However, if you're looking at a room with a total personality by-pass, it's not too late to establish a colour scheme by introducing coloured accessories. A confident combination of cushions and/or throws , rugs and carefully picked ornaments can introduce harmony and character. If you're unsure about which colour to use with another, consult the colour wheel (see opposite). Although you may favour energising bright colours from opposite sides, in this instance it would be wiser to use harmonising adjacent shades to create a calm and relaxing mood in the main rooms. Don't make the mistake of slapping on a coat of white paint as an easy solution. It can look bare and uncompromising and will subtly alter in shade, depending on the contents of the room and the light. Much better to go for soft neutrals and pastels which will blend with what's there, keeping the atmosphere without intruding on it.

- **Oil-based gloss — hard-wearing, shiny finish for woodwork, indoor and out.**
- **Oil-based eggshell — matt finish for interior woodwork.**
- **Acrylic gloss and eggshell are water-based variants. They're quick to dry, but not quite as hard-wearing as their oil-based relations.**
- **Primers and undercoats — use a primer and undercoat on any bare wood before applying your top coats.**
- **Water-based emulsion, silk or matt — for interior walls and ceilings.**
- **Solid emulsion — quick , easy and clean to use. Comes in its own tray. Non-drip, so good for ceilings, but costs more than regular emulsion.**
- **Specialist paints — if painting radiators, tiles or floors, make sure you get the appropriate paint. Ordinary emulsion or gloss won't stay put.**

SELL IT!

If the walls are bright, patterned or just plain ugly, paint them in light, neutral colours. The idea is to trick your potential buyers into visualising themselves living there. They just won't be able to do that if they're overwhelmed by the colour of the walls. Most people don't want to move into a house where they know they're immediately going to be involved in a heavy decorating job. If the background is neutral, then you can introduce splashes of colour with rugs, cushions, throws, table runners and flowers.

★**Above**: The colour wheel is an extremely useful tool when it comes to choosing paints. If you choose colours from the same side of the spectrum, they will blend naturally together, creating a soothing and harmonious atmosphere. However, if you want to create a more vibrant effect, pick colours that are opposite each other, being careful to use different strengths of tone so they complement one another rather than cancel each other out.

SOURCES

B&Q
Portswood House
1 Hampshire Corporate Park
Chandlers Ford
Hampshire SO53 3YX
Store location tel: 020 8466 4166
Website: www.dfy.com

Crown Decorative
Products Ltd
Crown House
Hollins Road
Darwen
Lancs BB3 0BG
Tel: 01254 704951

Dulux Paints
ICI Paint
Wexham Road
Slough
Berks SL2 5DS
Retail tel: 01753 556998
Trade tel: 01753 559991
Website: www.dulux.co.uk

International Tile
Paints
Plascon Int. Ltd
Brewery House
High Street
Twyford
Winchester SO21 1RG
Tel: 01962 711503
Website: www.plascon.co.uk

DIAGNOSIS
& cures

This room simply didn't look like a home. Where was its personality? The bare light bulbs and uncurtained windows did nothing for the feel. Nor did the amount of clutter accumulated on the small tables. Meanwhile, one end was just dead space with nothing going on in it whatsoever. Yellow cornicing drew the eye upwards, towards the offending lights. The room looked as if it was nothing more than an impersonal TV room for the two young bachelors who owned it.

dining area

What this town house lacked was a dining area. I felt that this might well put off a typical young professional buyer who would want to entertain at home. One end of the living room was unused and offered the ideal opportunity. Hiring furniture is a common thing in America and is possible here, too, so I had a sleek, contemporary glass-topped table with comfortable chairs delivered. It was then dressed with a few decorative items rather than leaving it bare. The coffee table was replaced with a pair of hired glass coffee tables which linked the two ends of the room.

window

Don't forget what's outside your house. The focal point of this room should have been the sensational view over the boats in Southampton marina. But it was just thrown away – having a window frame isn't enough on its own. The solution was a strong but simple window treatment. A pair of curtains to tone with the gold in the rest of the room framed the view perfectly. More than that, they broke up the harsh lines of the window frame and, adding a softness and fluidity of movement that was so notably absent before, they gave the room a more homely touch. The iron pole was deliberately longer than the window so that, when pulled back, the curtains didn't block either the view or the flow of light into the room. A streamlined uplighter, which stood to the left of the window, attracted the eye to that end of the room while, on the other side, the television was tucked neatly into the corner, the flowers distracting from its presence.

colour

By introducing a rich terracotta rug in the centre of the room to match the existing cushions, the room began to feel more centred and as if someone cared for it. The final warming touch was to paint the coving in the same colour.

case STUDY sold

"The cottage was a real jewel in the heart of London, but its location on a very busy main road was a big strike against it"

Wandsworth is an area of South London popular for its café culture. As in many areas of the city, the property market is hot, with most houses being snapped up within the first 48 hours of going on sale. Sean Mitchell and his girlfriend Kelly wanted to sell so they could start a beachfront health-food restaurant in Australia with the proceeds. Strangely, the hundred-year-old cottage had been on the market for six weeks without a bite. What could be wrong?

The cottage's position on a main road was enough to put off a lot of buyers. So once they'd stepped through the door, they had to be made to fall in love with the house immediately. Unfortunately, there was a lot of deferred maintenance, with many jobs left undone. It was like stepping into a hippy pad from the 1970s, which far from compensated for the road outside. The whole place needed lightening and brightening. First things first. Kelly took a week off work and stripped the whole house down (including taking up the tatty old living-room carpet) along with the *House Doctor* team. Meanwhile, procrastinator Sean had to finish all those tasks he'd begun, such as the tiling in the bathroom or painting the skirting in the kitchen. Both those rooms were very dark and dingy. We painted the wood ceilings white (immediately brightening them) and the walls with softer, more neutral colours.

Then it was just a question of adding the right accessories. The living area needed more work because you entered it on coming in from the street. It was large but scruffy and divided by an alarming, open slatted staircase. A coat of paint immediately improved things; cream for the walls and ceiling , with terracotta for the alcoves and shelves. Attaching some wooden dowelling between one side of the steps and the ceiling immediately gave the impression of some security on the stairs, as well as separating and defining the living and dining spaces without losing the room's open feeling. The floorboards were sanded and sealed. We put a pine fire surround (and removed the television!) from the old fireplace at the living end of the room and returned some authentic character to the cottage. The dining end of the room was simply and clearly defined by removing the fridge-freezer and Sean's bike, replacing them with a wine rack. We relocated their favourite things, adding some extra accessories and lighting — task lighting in the living area, with uplighters and a pendant lamp over the table in the dining area.

Upstairs the problem was the second bedroom, which was a disgrace. There were bare unplastered walls and a very uncomfortable-looking bed. But it wasn't hard to fix with paint and accessories.

Outside was a horribly neglected, tiny yard. Squashed between that busy road and a pub garden, it was essential that it be transformed into a sanctuary. In such an urban atmosphere, it's important to feel that there's somewhere to go and relax. Apart from clearing away all the rubbish that had accumulated there, we arranged a garden seat on each side and brought in lots of healthy plants. The *pièce de résistance* was a water feature which created a calming atmosphere and drowned out some of the noise.

Within a week we had made the whole place into a much more sophisticated and desirable home and, sure enough, Sean and Kelly swiftly secured an offer at the asking price.

photographs

Just seeing this corner of the living room tells you so much about the whole house. This was very much a family home where things had accumulated over the years. However, the trouble with selling your house is that you have to play this side of your life down, giving the rooms a neutral background so that your potential buyers can imagine how they will fit in. If your family are overwhelmingly in their face, then those are the only people they will ever be able to envisage there. One of the first jobs in this room was to remove all the family photographs and put them in safe keeping until they arrived at their new home.

pets

I would say that as many as fifty per cent of housebuyers don't like animals. When you're selling your house, you can't afford to let your pets hold their usual sway over the household — it's too much of a risk. All evidence of their existence must be lost. If you can get them to go and live with friends while you're selling your house, so much the better. If not, you'll have to change your lifestyle for that brief time. Gardens must be restored to as much of their former glory as possible. It's inside the house that you've got to be particularly careful. Hide any photos or prize-winning trophies. Now look at the surfaces. This living room was the comfortable home to a cat and a dog, so the carpet and furniture were covered with hairs. It needed a thorough shampoo. To lose the smell, open windows and buy pot-pourris and scented candles.

DIAGNOSIS
& cures

A working mother has no time to keep a show house. But the mayhem in this home, as reflected in the living room, was too much. Children and pets had taken their toll. The whole place was overwhelmed with the detritus of family life. We started with a thorough clean and the removal of all clutter and dead plants, before restoring the all-important focus to the fireplace.

shelving

Once the photographs had been removed, we could see what was actually on the shelves. It was still a muddle of books and ornaments which needed a good weeding out. Taking some items away and straightening those that were left immediately made things look better. Buried among them had been some attractive ornaments which could now be effectively displayed. The stereo system was compact enough not to draw undue attention to itself, if aligned on one of the lower shelves. Now we had achieved a message of order and elegance which was rather different from before! By tidying and styling the shelves on either side of the mantelpiece, the eye was no longer distracted from the real focal point of the room, the fireplace.

chair

A cosy chair by the fire is always inviting — except when it's covered in someone else's dog hairs! Always give it a doubly thorough brush and if necessary, wash any loose covers or have fitted ones steam-cleaned. Toss a coloured cushion into the picture and you've added an extra note of comfort plus, as in this case, linked the chair to the green rug that we chose to set a keynote for the room.

prescription ACCESSORIES

Once you've achieved that all-important neutral background, largely by eliminating bold colours and patterns, or too many contrasting colours on the walls of a room, it's time to look at the accessories you can use to build colour back in. Accessories can carry a colour theme through your house, pulling the look of each room together. You must ruthlessly remove all the expendable bits and pieces and only replace with things that are essential to the look. Check in the back of your cupboards. I've seen forgotten wedding gifts come into their own at this moment. If you are really stuck, it's time for a bit of retail therapy — after all anything you buy will go with you to your new home. Go easy though, you don't want to confuse your buyer into thinking they've walked into a bazaar. Cushions, throws and ornaments may brighten up a living room in moderation, while fluffy towels, new soaps and a shower curtain can transform a bathroom. You may want to colour-coordinate a <u>few</u> items on the kitchen worktop — matching kettle, toaster and jars for tea, coffee and sugar can jolly things up. New candles look good in almost every room and, of course, candlesticks can reflect the style of the house, traditional or modern, and be used to introduce colour, too. Use large pictures or a mirror on a blank wall. Accessories make the difference between a bland, uninteresting house and a vital, desirable home.

- **Clear all clutter.**
- **Choose the colour scheme you want to develop.**
- **Rediscover what there is in the house and use things in a different way.**
- **Shop for a few essentials that will pull the look of a room together.**
- **Tread a fine line between unlived-in and overcrowded.**
- **Replace worn accessories such as towels, tea towels and bits of soap.**
- **Replace tired or torn lampshades to colour-match the room.**

SELL IT!

The first and most essential rule for every home staging is to clear the clutter. Mess all too easily becomes familiar junk which we are used to having around. But it gives the wrong impression of a room. It makes it look smaller and sends unhelpful messages to your buyers. You must make it as easy as possible for them to imagine themselves living here with their things. Tidy away family photos and books. If you can't find space to store the less personal stuff, throw it in the boot of your car and take as much as possible to the nearest dump.

SOURCES

Ikea Ltd
2 Drury Way
North Circular Road
London NW10 0JO
Tel: 020 8280 5600
Website: www.ikea.com

David Cook Pottery
Spring Cottage
Church Street
Upwey
Weymouth
Dorset DT3 5QE
Tel: 01305 812665

The Factory Shop
The Foreman Centre
High Street
Headcorn
Kent TN27 9NE
Tel: 01622 891651

Take Cover
142 Church Street
London NW8 8EX
Tel: 020 7258 1171

From top to bottom: Colourful cushions and throws make the perfect finishing touch and can transform the appearance of a room. ★ Don't underestimate the effect of fluffy new towels and bathmats. They add colour and a welcome touch of luxury. ★ Check that you've thrown away all those unfinished old bits of soap and buy some beautifully scented replacements. ★
Far left: The look of a room can be pulled together by coordinating the curtains and cushions, or throws and cushions.

^{the}CURE

clutter

This room was transformed simply by losing the small, unmatching table which had become the centre for all useless items, dirty cups and sheets of paper. A new, smarter, contemporary table with matching white telephone proved inexpensive and highly effective.

flooring

The brown carpet was horribly drab and dull. Unfortunately, the floorboards underneath weren't quite good enough to sand and varnish. However, a useful alternative is to paint them with specialist paint. Check that there aren't any nails sticking out and that the surface is smooth, clean and dry before you apply it. You won't believe the difference.

furniture

You're not going to sell your house if it looks like a pigsty. The new coffee table looked more contemporary than the last and doubled as a cunning CD storage unit. All the rest of the clutter was hidden in a useful pine cupboard. Its lines were softened by a delicate runner and lights. The reflections in the mirror create the illusion of more space and light.

curtains

There's nothing worse than grubby old net curtains, especially when teamed with ugly floral curtains that don't fit the window. The nets were replaced by Venetian blinds which fulfil the same function of maintaining privacy, while letting the sunshine in. They were teamed with floaty, muslin curtains to frame the window and tie in with the colour scheme.

before

after

the CURE

modernise

The messages given by this room were muddled. The Victorian fireplace sat uneasily beside the modern shelves and furniture. A new colour scheme dramatically altered the whole feel, transforming it into something much more consistently up-to-date and appealing.

accessories

Although it's said that books furnish a room, they're not the only things that look good on shelves. To underline the new, contemporary style of the room, accessories were chosen especially to tone in with the colour scheme. A few silver and chrome photo frames and lamp bases are set off by the delicate blue glass. Even gin and vodka bottles can be used decoratively!

fireplace

The Victorian fire surround didn't fit in with the new look at all. The solution was radical. Specialist paints did the trick of hiding the tiles and transforming the whole thing into a funky, modern fireplace which blended with the overall look of the room.

clutter

Get rid of it! A cuddly teddy bear may have been the owner's idea of cuteness but it won't impress potential buyers who would rather see a streamlined, clutter-free home. Again, the junk was moved from the bookcase and from the mantelpiece, allowing the room to breathe.

before

the CURE

floor

For a no-nonsense minimalist look, that hideous green carpet was for the dump. Losing the carpet from the wooden floor immediately gave the room a lighter, more up-to-the-minute look. It could easily be warmed up with the addition of a colourful rug or two.

light

White walls can look great, but if you're not careful it can be like living inside an ice palace. Accenting one wall as a large block of colour warmed the room without losing the sense of space and light. Rather than having heavy curtains blocking the windows, coloured net let the light in, while simultaneously allowing the shape of the window to be seen.

shelving

Shelving breaks up empty wall space. It doesn't have to be crammed with all your worldly possessions — why not use it as a showcase for your favourite things? These box shelves were straightforward to make and, painted white, they made a strong visual statement as they ran side by side along one wall.

lighting

The way you light a room can make the world of difference to it. A mobile, standard Anglepoise lamp was used as an uplighter to create ambient glow. A dimmer switch was installed for creating different moods. Alternatively, it could be used as a task light to shed light over the table for meals, or over an armchair for easy reading.

54 | **House Doctor**

before

after

Chapter Four
KITCHENS

The kitchen is probably the biggest selling ticket you've got, so make the most of it. Your buyers must be made to feel that this is a room in which they'll want to spend time, without having to spend money remodelling it.

As with every room, the first thing to do is remove ALL superficial clutter, including the jolly magnetic letters from the fridge door and the sheaf of notices from the pinboard. Evidence of your children and hectic social life may make you feel good, but it focuses the buyer's eyes on the wrong things. Then you must clean, clean and clean again.

Don't forget the floor. Assuming that it isn't too bad, simply and cheaply replace worn or dirty lino. A rug might brighten it up, but not near where you cook. Too much will be dropped on it too quickly and you'll have to replace it.

These days, people tend to want light, bright, spacious kitchens. If you have used a strong wall colour, it would be wise to repaint in a much more muted tone, either subtly echoing the colour in the splashback tiles or the curtains, or with a safe neutral colour. Similarly, if the units are dark, dated and intrusive, they will benefit from being painted a neutral white or cream. If they are looking really tatty, it may be worth replacing the doors or, at the very least, the handles. Ensure that doors shut properly.

Work space is at a premium. Double check that you've cleared the worktops of all inessential items, though a bowl of fruit or a vase of flowers can make a nice finishing touch. If your kitchen table is showing signs of knife score marks, disguise them with a tablecloth or a length of colourful PVC. Make sure that the waste bin is empty. There's nothing more off-putting than rubbish spilling out all over the place. Take care of any laundry that might be piled up waiting to be washed or ironed.

All your appliances should be in working order. Pay attention to minor repairs, fix hinges, fasten the handle on the oven door, fix the door on the washing machine and get a new washer for that dripping tap. These are psychological red flags that can lead a buyer to conclude that you are careless about looking after other things in your home as well.

You may have sunshine flooding the room during the day, but what about in the evening when many prospective buyers will visit? All your working areas should be properly lit. It won't cost much to buy a simple tracking system which can be directed at various points. Unpleasant cooking odours are another no-no. It's been said before, but the smell of baking bread or a fresh pot of coffee does wonders for creating an impression of homeliness. However, if you are culinarily challenged, then a simple vanilla pod placed in a warm oven will have the same effect.

Now you have created a kitchen which is not only clean and inviting, it's also functioning properly, looks as spacious as it possibly can, and is ready for the next owner to move in.

DIAGNOSIS
& cures

Far from being the major selling point a kitchen should be, this room was a mess. Every surface had something on it that should have been removed. Buyers want to see the full expanse of work surface, not the colour of your sheets or how many people were drinking wine last night. The overall impression was one of a gloomy corridor which led through to another door. It was my job to redefine it by making it feel like a self-contained room with one purpose. We moved the fridge from the living room and introduced some much-needed light and life by repairing the uncompleted DIY and emphasising the window.

clean up

The door to the washing machine was open, giving a clear message to the owner. Washing, clean or dirty, must be put away and all appliance doors shut. That old towel at the end of the units does nothing for the room either. The washing up on the draining board was firmly put where it belonged and homes were found for every single inessential item that was littering the worktops. The only exception was the finishing touch of an attractive bowl containing fruit, which made it look as though the kitchen was being used and not just a showroom.

lighten up

First to go was the old-fashioned tongue-and-groove ceiling, transformed with a serious application of white paint. Then, to cheer the room, we chose a pale green for the walls which toned with the decorative tiles. Mysteriously, part of the window frame had been left as varnished wood – though not for any longer! Finally, out went the dated wood blind and in came a bright white roman blind which didn't obscure the window or block the light. The simple trick of hanging a curtain to hide the next door made the kitchen feel enclosed and properly defined – at last it was its own space.

DIY – now!

When you're selling your house, you must attend to all those jobs that you've been meaning to tackle for months. Unfinished repairs can give the impression that there are others not so obvious to the naked eye. Both the skirting board and the plasterwork above it in this kitchen were unpainted, which would immediately set alarm signals sounding in a buyer's mind. Do the decent thing and paint it.

storage

The kitchen is one room where storage is vital. Pots and pans hanging from the wall only add to a general sense of chaos and an impression that there's no room to put anything. Although there were some existing shelves and utensil hooks, they smacked too much of student DIY and were too solid to be doing the room any favours in terms of space. These slatted shelves are a better solution. They use the dead space on one wall and are less heavy and obtrusive. The hooks below are just the place for tea towels – new ones!

DIAGNOSIS
& cures

This was one of the smallest kitchens I've ever been in. Working on a budget, we couldn't refit a new one to make better use of the space, so the only alternative was to make the most of what we had. Streamlining a small space can be surprisingly effective so, as with many other kitchens, the first thing to attend to was the general untidiness. The strong colour scheme was replaced with white. Replacing the existing flooring with blue tiles completed the look.

work top

Work surfaces are at a premium, particularly in a kitchen this size. By clearing all of the inessentials away, the space was exposed and it appeared as if there was enough storage capacity. The Formica tops were well used, so were reinvigorated with specialist white paint.

wash up

The focal point of this room was the washing up. Scrappy old tea towels hung on the radiator (beware, they can smell, too), upturned mugs and glasses on the draining board and the ugliest thing of all, a washing-up liquid container on the window sill, made the kitchen look cluttered and small. It was not difficult to put everything away and add an attractive fern.

space

It was essential to create the illusion of space here. We cleared the surfaces and changed the shelving to make it less intrusive. The walls became brilliant white, providing a striking contrast with the blue, maximising the sense of space.

prescription
DOORS

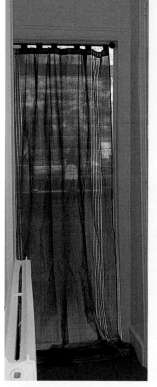

A door can be a strong focal point. It is the architectural feature that introduces you to the space behind it and gives the first clue to what you might find there. Make a feature of your front door. If it is painted the same colour as the windows, it will lose impact. Much better to choose a strong colour, matching the frame with the window frames. Bear in mind the colour of your neighbours' doors, too – clashing colours can look awful. Painting your door doesn't cost much and can lift the appearance of the exterior of your house.

Apart from dividing one room from another and maintaining privacy between those spaces, doors can also be decorative. They can break up the monotony of a wall. Would your door look better if the frame or the panels were a different colour? Alternatively, if the walls are busy, you might want the door to blend into the background by painting it the same colour as the wall or extending bookshelves to run over the top of it. Don't block doors with pieces of furniture. It's important that the flow of the home is efficient, making any newcomer feel more comfortable there. Ask yourself if all the doors are absolutely essential. An archway may be as effective. Consider a tie-back curtain on an iron rod – it can be both elegant and space-saving. Or you might replace door panels with glazing. You'd be surprised how a dingy hallway can be made lighter and much less claustrophobic, even if you use etched, smoked or coloured glass.

Check that the style of your doors suits the period of your house.
All door furniture should match and be polished thoroughly.
Replace fittings with the simplest style if you're uncertain.
Make sure everything about the door works – hinges, bell, handle etc.
Decorate interior doors – contrasting panels and beading; stencilling on the frame or panels.
Don't block doors with furniture or clutter.
If a door isn't essential, remove it and make an archway, eradicating all signs of the hinges, which are easy to forget.

SELL IT!

Make sure all entrances are uncluttered, warm and welcoming. Mark the path to your front door with potted plants on either side. Or you may want to flank a door or french windows with single plant pots or hanging baskets. Make sure the doors open properly and aren't hampered by a row of coats or muddy boots behind. Check that furniture doesn't stop any of the internal doors from opening or shutting properly. Draughts and a sense of everything being squashed into a room won't hasten your chances of a sale.

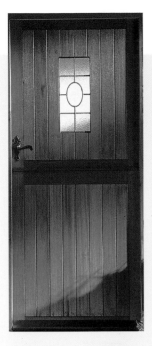

Clockwise, left to right: A small window in a front door can make a difference to a dark hallway ★ Door fittings that match gleam in welcome on this traditional panelled front door ★ If a door is constantly left open, it may make sense to remove it altogether and create a feature of the resulting archway ★ Ensure your doors match the period of your home and give them a kiss of life with a new coat of paint ★ **Far left**: A sheer curtain covering a doorway into a dark hallway can both lighten the hall and keep the kitchen area separate.

SOURCES

'Er in Doors
35 Beech Road
St Albans
Herts
Tel: 01727 811921
Fax: 01727 858026

Homebase
Beddington House
Railway Approach
Wallington
Surrey SM6 0HB
Tel: 020 8784 7200
Website: www.homebase.co.uk

The Magnet Co.
Royd Ings Road
Keighley
Yorks BD21 4BY
Tel: 01535 661133
Fax: 01535 662896

Marshall Tufflex Ltd
Ponswood
Hastings TN34 1YJ
Tel: 01424 427691

case STUDY

> "On walking in, you were bombarded with colour. It was too male, too personal and made far too bold a statement. Things had to change"

Steve Power bought his house seven years ago. It had been an ideal bachelor pad, then his fiancée Jean Wiseman moved in. Now their plans were to sell both their homes and buy somewhere to start a new life together. Jean's house had sold immediately whereas Steve's had been languishing on the market for the last nine months. Knutsford is a picturesque market town which is popular with people commuting to Manchester. Steve's part-rendered mid-terrace cottage should have been snapped up as quickly as Jean's had. What was wrong?

He had painted the living room a bright yellow and blue. His bedroom was a vivid lemon yellow and was crowded with all of Jean's possessions that she needed to store after moving out of her house. It looked as if there wasn't any storage space in Steve's home. On the other hand, he hadn't touched the kitchen since moving in. It was dated, tired and bland with its dark wood units, scuffed lino and dreary wall colours. The bathroom was pretty dull, too, plus Jean told us she was anxious that potential buyers would be put off by the fact that it was downstairs.

Apart from tidying everything up, my job was to take Steve's stamp off the place and create an environment where other people might imagine themselves living. The colours had to go if the house was ever going to sell.

"Jean and I edited Steve's possessions. We didn't want the house to look stripped, so we had to tread a fine line between too much and not enough. Everything must count"

A large part of our budget was spent on the kitchen. I wanted to brighten the neutral atmosphere so that it would appeal to most people. We levelled the floor and put down some new lino and then painted the cupboards a paler colour and the walls a natural warm shade. A couple of toning rugs and some food-related pictures finished it off.

The first job in the living room was to clear up and sort out. Then we repainted with a more restful shade of yellow and eliminated the blue trim altogether. The grubby old shag-pile carpet was a must for the garbage, so down went a brand-new carpet in a lighter shade. Finally I showed them the importance of paying attention to the main spaces of the room and making a feature of them. Steve must have had his entire CD collection and all his books crammed into one corner, so we thinned them out.

We transformed the acid yellow of the bedroom into something more muted. Using the colour scheme they'd started with, we went from there. The finishing touch was to add a new duvet which picked up the colours of the windows and walls, bringing the whole thing together.

It wasn't the location of the bathroom that was the problem. All we had to do was change the way it looked by giving it a good clean, freeing it of clutter and then adding coordinating blinds, curtains, bathmat, towels, soaps and other accessories.

With Steve's taste obliterated, the house now presented a blank canvas ready for the next owners to create their own personality.

the CURE

brighten up

This kitchen reminded me of bed-sit days. A light, contemporary paint treatment soon overcame its personality by-pass and the room began to look as though it could be enjoyed again.

window

The view outside wasn't so great, but a kitchen needs as much light as it can possibly get. A simple but effective solution was to use a thin fabric blind which took the edge off what was beyond it, adding a softness to the room, while not depriving it of any natural light.

update

Galvanised metal sheeting transformed the whole look of this kitchen. Easily attached to the unit doors, it immediately made them stylishly modern. A small but fashionable Shaker-style cupboard filled the dead wall space, its mesh door allowing a sense of space to be retained there.

style it

An empty kitchen looks unused and unloved. Although I always recommend clearing clutter, very occasionally it helps to leave some around — but the tidier the better! Flowers always look attractive and help to create a fresh, natural look.

before

after

the CURE

make the most

Only the most princely budget would allow someone to splash out on new kitchen fittings before they moved. The only thing to be done here was to cheer up that lifeless grey and make sure that there was something in the room to distract attention from the rather dull run of units.

decorate

It's true that grey was once the must-have colour, but in this kitchen it looked depressing and of its time. Not even the yellow coving jollied it up. Repainting in a warm apricot transformed the place into somewhere any of us would want to be.

define

The kitchen is for cooking, not watching television, so the TV was removed. The table was moved to the other side of the room, giving the illusion that there was a separate space within the room, clearly defined for eating in.

aromas

Laying the table to issue a subliminal invitation is one thing. But you can also combine it with delicious cooking smells. And I mean delicious — not yesterday's chips. If you're not up to a casserole, buy some half-baked bread and finish it off in the oven with some freshly made coffee on the side. You'll be surprised how seductive it can be.

before

LIGHTS & SWITCHES

Lighting can make an enormous difference to the appearance of a room. A bare light bulb swinging from the ceiling not only looks awful, it makes everything else in the room look awful, too. So, before you go any further, look at the lighting you have and see how it can be improved. Dusty, tired or faded lampshades should be replaced immediately. Alternatives do not have to be expensive or elaborate, but they will certainly improve the look of the room. It may be better to go for a warmer, creamy shade than a white one which can create a much colder effect. Or you might consider swapping a standard daytime bulb with a warm-toned bulb (red or orange), which will give a completely different sort of light. Central ceiling lights in a living room or bedroom are never as complimentary or as atmospheric as a range of table lamps or a pair of bedside lamps which will be much softer. Where possible, angle the light so that it falls on areas used for activities in the room and hides the bits you'd rather weren't seen. In the kitchen it's important to ensure that your working areas are adequately lit. Clip-on spotlights or a track of halogen downlighters may be a worthwhile investment. Candlelight can be both flattering and dramatic. Throw out any half-burned stubs and arrange new candles to give some extra atmosphere. Nor is it expensive to replace your switches with dimmers, which give you the advantage of being able to alter the strength of lighting in the room to suit the time of day.

Look at cleaning up existing light fittings before investing in new ones.
If you are going to replace, first define your period.
Decide whether you're going with authentic or repro materials.
Use officially approved materials.
● Ensure that all wiring is sound.
Shop around for your switches and light fittings. The first ones you find are not always the best or the cheapest.
Use a properly qualified electrician.

SELL IT!

A favourite trick of mine is to use a mirror wherever I can. Apart from adding space to a room, a carefully placed mirror also maximises the available light. Ensure that it is hung at eye level — it may sound obvious, but it's not always done. Check there is a well-lit mirror in your bathroom. You can make the world of difference to a dark entrance hall with a strategically placed mirror. Hung over a fireplace, one often makes the ideal finishing touch to the focal point of the room. Placing a candle in front of a mirror creates an extra light source.

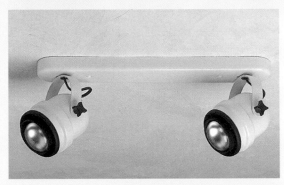

Christopher Wray

591–593 Kings Road

London SW6 2YW

Catalogue tel: 020 7384 2888

Enquiries tel: 020 7736 8434

Website:

www.christopherwray.com

B & Q

Portswood House

1 Hampshire Corporate Park

Chandlers Ford

Hampshire SO53 3YX

Head office tel: 01703 256256

Store location tel: 020 8466 4166

Website: www.dfy.com

Habitat UK Ltd

196 Tottenham Court Road

London W1P 9LD

Tel: 020 7255 2545

Website: www.habitat.co.uk

Ikea Ltd

London tel: 020 8208 5600

Croydon tel: 020 8208 5601

Leeds tel: 01924 423296

Thurrock tel: 01708 860868

Website: www.ikea.com

Clockwise, left to right: An uplighter is a good way of achieving ambient light ★ A single spot is useful for highlighting a particular area or object ★ A downlighter is another way of providing ambient light ★ A tracking system of halogen spotlights is ideal for lighting a kitchen ★ Choose your switches to suit the period and style of your home. There is a huge range to choose from ★ Three spots can simultaneously light different areas of the same room. ★ **Far left:** A standard lamp and a table lamp provide useful background lighting.

the CURE

finish off

The room needed a thorough clean and tidy. The area below the tiles had never been finished and the gaping hole by the washing machine was an eyesore. The problem was solved by moving it and installing the boiler in its place.

glass

The blind did nothing to disguise the grim view outside the window. Cutting circles in frosted adhesive sheet which was then stuck on the lower panes solved the problem and added a fun aspect.

décor

Fussy details do nothing for a busy room. The blind was removed altogether. Instead of wallpaper, the walls were painted an intense shade of deep orange while the units were freshened up with a contrasting shade of blue.

modernise

The old floor tiles had seen better days. For a funky new look, deep blue tiles were laid to provide contrast with the walls and units. The look was completed by dressing the chairs in matching blue covers.

before

theCURE

crowding

Packing a table into a kitchen this size is madness. It means there is neither room for cooking nor for eating. The table blocks the natural flow of movement round the kitchen and makes the room impossibly busy.

blinds

White venetian blinds were a perfect window treatment here. They let in light but could provide privacy without interfering with the lines of the room. Easy to take down and washable, they will maintain their smart appearance for years.

floorboards

The floorboards looked tired and scuffed once the room had been repainted. One solution would have been to lime them, but painting them white provided a practical and effective treatment. Specialist floor paint was a must — anything else will not take the inevitable wear and tear.

simplicity

The clean and simple lines of the new kitchen were in total contrast with its dated and messy predecessor. The most basic worktop provided space underneath for the fridge and mobile storage units. Painting the whole room white left no hostages to dust and provided a bright, exhilarating finish.

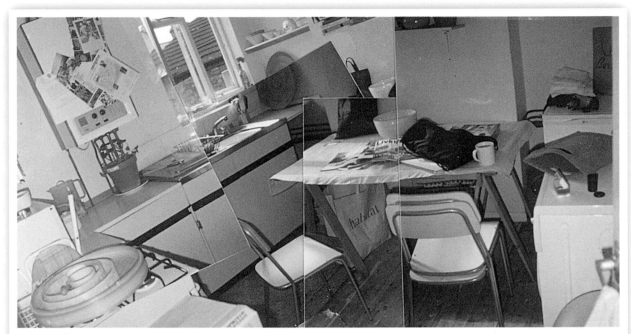

before

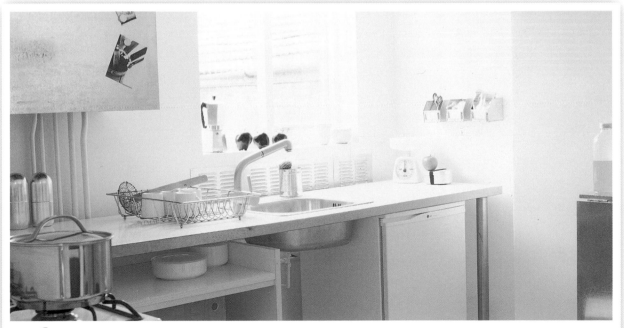

after

"A buyer won't want a
room which leaves their
nerves jangling"

Chapter Five
BEDROOMS

When staging your house for sale, remember the importance of the master bedroom. A buyer won't want a room which leaves their nerves jangling from unexpected combinations of bright colours, nor one that gives the impression of being a storeroom with a bed squeezed in a corner. Once again, it's a question of clearing all that clutter out of the way. Remember, you are creating the illusion of space and calm.

Having cleared the room, look at it objectively. What will the colours say to another person? It only takes a couple of pots of paint to turn an idiosyncratic choice of wallpaper into something more neutral. A fresh new rug can add a splash of colour to the room, as well as cover up any bits of carpet that have seen better days.

Double check that your bed is in the best position it could be. Make sure that there's access to it from both sides and, if possible, that it faces towards the window, particularly if there's a good view. If, for some reason, the bed base is resting on the floor, attach its legs or raise it on bricks hidden by a valance. Otherwise it looks too much like a student pad. A new bedspread or duvet can do wonders for brightening up the room too, particularly if combined with some colourful cushions.

If you haven't got a bedside table, either buy one cheaply (an MDF flat pack with a pretty table cover is easy and inexpensive), or remove your alarm clock and glass of water from the floor. Make sure that your wardrobe and chest of drawers shut properly, otherwise the room will look untidy, destroying the tranquillity you are striving to convey.

Lighting in a bedroom is always important. Make sure that a pendant light is complemented by bedside lights for reading as well as for extra light. Clean the windows, perhaps drawing attention to them by replacing tired curtains or adding a blind. They should tie in with the bedding.

It's important to create a focal point, too. If you have a fireplace in the room, make sure it suits the period of the house. If it's boxed in then have the courage to reinstate it. Grates and surrounds can be found at architectural salvage yards for reasonable prices. If you are not using a fire or candles in the grate, then a firescreen or a dried flower arrangement can smarten it up. Hanging a mirror above the mantelpiece will draw attention to that wall and increase the sense of space and light in the room. Alternatively, it's the perfect place to hang a favourite picture.

This is the one room where, when selling your house, I allow personal photographs. So invest in some pretty frames and use them on your bedside table or mantel. Finally, don't forget those finishing touches — a bowl of pot pourri, a vase of fresh flowers, some colourful prints — which always make a big difference.

detail

Unlike in the early days of central heating when redundant fireplaces were boxed in, now they are appreciated for their period worth. Not only that, but they provide a wonderful focal point to a room whether or not they're used. Before redecorating, we removed the box that hid the hole where the fireplace had once been. We found an appropriate Victorian fireplace with surround in an architectural salvage yard. Painted white, it completely transformed the feel of the room, giving it an elegance that had previously been missing.

DIAGNOSIS
& cures

The wallpaper in this bedroom took my breath away. It was essential that we toned it down so that any potential buyer could consider the merits of the room uninterrupted. The owners had decided to box in the hole left when the original fireplace was removed and paper over it. A big mistake, in my view. Most people want as many original features as possible when they are buying a period home. It's almost always advisable to restore or replace them if you can. The bed looked as if it had been made in a hurry and the amount of clutter made the room feel claustrophobic and cramped.

wallpaper

The vivid chintz wallpaper in this room was overwhelming.
A pattern as strong as this can be extremely off-putting to
potential buyers. If they don't like it, then they'll leave
convinced that redecorating is one more unwanted job that's
going to have to be done on moving in. Why put these ideas in their
head when it's not expensive to redecorate yourself? We chose a warm
terracotta emulsion which showed off the dark wood furniture and the fire surround. It also had the
benefit of making the room seem larger and certainly more relaxing.

make your bed

A properly made bed with white sheets couldn't be more inviting. We replaced the existing bed
linen with something uncrumpled and much smarter. I felt that the pillows and back cushion
looked very untidy, so suggested buying a single bolster which would give support while reading in bed,
but be less messy. By sticking to white, which went with the skirtings, ceiling and fireplace, we achieved a
unified impression of peace and calm. The bedside tables and the floor were cleared of anything that wasn't absolutely
essential, to give as much of a sense of space as possible.

colour scheme

Starting from scratch certainly has its advantages, but I decided to go with the blues and greens that the couple already had in the room. After thoroughly preparing the wall, we painted it a soft apple green. The old paper lantern was replaced by a toning green shade which cast a soft glow. Using the bedspread as the basis for other colours, I chose scatter cushions and a throw to disguise the old blue sofa. As for "blue and green should never be seen", as you can see, if you're careful with the shades they can look terrific.

DIAGNOSIS
& cures

The diagnosis was straightforward enough: the bedroom had never been finished. It's one of those DIY jobs that had been left because the house was being sold. But my guess was that, in fact, it was one of the reasons why the house wasn't selling. There was a marked air of general neglect and the room left too many question marks in a viewer's mind. Leaking roof? Damp? As for the unpleasant-looking bedding and the paper light shade, of course they had to be replaced before an injection of life began.

window

If you have a large window, it's often a good idea to make a feature of it. In this case, once the frame had been properly treated and painted, I could think about how to dress it. The old-fashioned split-cane blind was replaced with a lighter fabric one which covered the entire window, disguising the uninspiring view yet letting in as much light as possible. We deliberately made the curtain pole longer than the window so that when the pale full-length curtains were drawn back, the whole window was visible and no light was blocked from coming in.

furniture

An empty room looks uncared-for and uninspiring. It's never a good idea to have the furniture pushed back against the walls, so I turned the bed into the room to face the fireplace, which is much more pleasant to look at than a blank wall. A chest of drawers and a small bookshelf suggested that the room was lived in and that there was space for storage, while the sofa was given a cheap new lease of life with a throw. With plants, pictures and scented candles the room was transformed.

colour scheme

There was nothing wrong with the colour the owner had chosen for the walls. She just hadn't followed it through into the room to make a coherent statement. The original bedspread did nothing for the room, so we replaced it with one that picked up the blue of the walls. We piled up cushions whose colours tied in with those of the bedspread, to create an opulent yet comfy effect. The finishing touches were the white candles and a white bedside light which echoed the brilliant white of the paintwork.

DIAGNOSIS
& cures

This room was painted an attractive shade of blue but it needed dressing up to give it the character it sadly lacked. The owner had a humidifier in a corner which gave the wrong message to any potential buyer, suggesting the room perhaps had a damp problem. Once we'd cleared the clutter away, it was time to rearrange the furniture to make the most of the space, and add some dramatic final touches. I wanted the feel of the room to fit in with the Victorian gothic style of the rest of the apartment.

mirror

One of my favourite tricks worked like a dream here. A large mirror added space and light to a rather small room. The ornate gold-painted frame went with the gothic look I was trying to achieve. I doubled the number of candles burning in front of a mirror, which enhanced the slightly eerie effect I wanted.

bedhead

The main addition to the room was the splendid gothic-style "headboard" which looked grand, but which was simply painted on the wall. This is a trick that needs to be done extremely carefully, however, or it can look a complete mess. It's also important that the design of the headboard is in keeping with the rest of your house. So it's not a solution that will easily suit any bedroom. If you are the slightest bit unsure about your artistic talents, then ask a professional to do it for you. You won't regret it.

define the space

Always make it as easy as possible for your potential buyer to see exactly what a room, or an area of a room, is used for. Your house is competing with others on the market in your area and every bit of it needs to be presented at its best. An empty room is a sorry sight. It doesn't look like a room with potential but just gives the impression of lack of care. We could have made this room into a dressing room or a study, but because there was only one other bedroom in the house, it was better to present it as a second bedroom. Besides, the wardrobes were already there.

DIAGNOSIS
& cures

It didn't need a house doctor to see what was wrong with this room. It was empty! Because there was no furniture to distract the eye, the yellow décor was horribly overpowering. It was essential to define the purpose of the room to help viewers to imagine themselves living there. Besides, an obvious second bedroom can only add value to a house. Understandably, the owner didn't want to spend a fortune furnishing the room, so I was able to show him he didn't have to.

pictures

A couple of squint pictures only added to the unloved aspect of this room.
Replacing them with four new ones, carefully hung, made all the difference. You
don't have to spend a fortune to achieve the same effect. If you don't want to buy
ready-framed pictures, you can frame postcards or cheap prints in inexpensive,
ready-made frames. More inventively, mount a leaf or feather on coloured paper.

bed

The obvious thing missing was the bed. These can, of course, be extremely expensive,
but as we were concerned with selling the house and not getting a good night's sleep,
we went to a second-hand shop and bought one of the cheapest we could find. It may
not have looked much to start with, but once we'd made it up with fresh new bed linen,
nobody would spot the difference. Inexpensive bedside tables and lights were the
finishing touches to the room, which now looked as if it had a purpose.

prescription
WINDOWS

If any of your windows are beyond repair you should replace them. It may seem a big job but it will make a difference to your sale. Whatever you do, make sure that the replacements are as close to the originals as possible. However, it is more likely that what you will be faced with is some minor repairs. All the paintwork should be touched up where necessary and washed where not. On the exterior of the house, it is safest to go for clean white gloss on the window frames, making sure that all the windows open and close properly. They can be decorated by using window boxes, provided they are well-planted and colourful. Make sure any curtains or blinds you can see from outside are clean and properly hung.

When staging a house, it's important to look outside "the box", too. If there is a particularly good view then draw attention to it by dressing the appropriate window. Curtains don't need to be expensive or elaborate to be effective and they can add colour to the room. Make sure they blend with the general scheme and draw back to let in as much light as possible. Try not to hide the shape of an unusual and attractively designed window. Shabby old net curtains are one of my pet hates. If you want to retain privacy and light, the best solution is to invest in blinds. Venetian blinds are one effective choice but roman blinds can be made in fine cotton or voile, which are more feminine and play the same trick. If the view's dire, you might want a curtain which covers the bottom half of the window only.

Clean all windows until they sparkle.
Wash the paintwork round them.
Ensure that they all open and shut properly.
Check that all window furniture matches and works.
Investigate the different kinds of blinds on the market.
Don't block the flow of sunlight into the room.

SELL IT!

Remember all those little jobs round the house that you've always meant to finish? Now's the time to do it. If you realise that the reason for the delay is because you don't really know what you're doing, then get someone in who does. It won't be expensive and it's vital to selling your house. Broken window catches, a front door bell that doesn't work or half-finished shelves convey an air of neglect and signal to a potential buyer that there may be other, more significant aspects of the house that have been left undone.

Right, top to bottom: Leaded glass should always be clean to allow maximum possible light ★ Glass doors leading to the garden must be kept spotlessly clean. It's important not to block access to them ★ You may want to lighten a dark hall, but remember that, if the solution is as extreme as this, you must keep the inside extremely tidy ★ All paintwork should be touched up where necessary and curtains should be clean and hung properly. ★ **Far left:** plastic-coated aluminium frames need to be carefully cleaned and, if necessary, repaired. Blinds should be straight and evenly displayed ★ **Below:** stained or patterned glass can be a cheap, effective way of beautifying an entrance.

SOURCES

Marshall Tufflex Ltd
Ponswood
Hastings TN34 1YJ
Tel: 01424 427691

B & Q
Portswood House
1 Hampshire Corporate Park
Chandlers Ford
Hampshire SO53 3YX
Head office tel: 01703 256256
Store location tel: 020 8466 4166
Website: www.dfy.com

Homebase
Beddington House
Railway Approach
Wallington
Surrey SM6 0HB
Tel: 020 8784 7200
Website: www.homebase.co.uk

BLINDS
Tidmarsh
32 Hyde Way
Welwyn Garden City
Herts AL7 3AW
Tel: 01707 886226
Fax: 01707 886227
Website: www.bbsa\uk.com.com

the CURE

chaos

Clutter on such a grand scale is far from conducive to a good night's sleep. Before anything was done to this room, it had to be thoroughly cleared and cleaned.

workspace

If a bedroom has to double as an office then it's wise to build in some furniture that can be used as desk and storage. There are so many attractive storage boxes and filing systems around that there's no excuse for untidiness.

walls

The lifeless wall colour was changed to a smart blue which immediately lifted the room and brought it bang up to date. The deliberate absence of pictures contrasted strongly with its previous incarnation and now promotes a feeling of calm.

floor

The stripped wooden floor has a strong finish which is cheaper to reveal than recarpeting and can look just as good. Bear in mind who's below, though. If the sound of you pacing your workplace isn't muffled by carpet they may be less than pleased.

before

after

"Old dog-ends of soap
stuck to the side of the
basin are a grim sight"

Chapter Six
BATHROOMS

Although the bathroom comes a long way behind the kitchen as a selling ticket on a house, it is absolutely essential that it gets the same treatment. If you can't keep it clean and tidy for yourself, then at least make the effort while you are trying to sell the house.

First of all, you must do your best to make the room as clean as you possibly can. It's amazing what a little elbow grease can do. Clean the bath, basin and lavatory for all you are worth, right down to the hairs that are caught in the plughole. Clean the grouting between the tiles and remove any limescale from them. If any are loose or missing, splash out on a small tub of tile cement and stick them back in place.

Prospective buyers won't be taken with any inventive colour schemes, so consider painting the walls a pale colour, a soft blue or a primrose yellow, so that the room appears light and clean. Double check the flooring, too. Curling linoleum is a turn-off, as is a grubby bit of carpet covered with toothpaste stains. It may well be worthwhile replacing it — new lino which is stuck down properly will be ideal.

Remove all the clutter, including your well-used toothbrush and squashed-up toothpaste tube. Nobody wants to know what deodorant you use or any other details of your ablutions — get rid of what you can and hide the rest in a medicine cabinet on the wall. Old dog-ends of soap stuck to the side of the basin are a grim sight. Bin them and replace with a deliciously smelly new substitute.

Is the shower curtain hanging sleekly on all its hooks or looking forlorn and water-marked? Splash out on a new one, making sure you hang it properly.

Light in the bathroom is essential. If you have a windowless room, make sure there is a decent light by a mirror so that shaving and make-up can be done painlessly and realistically. If you want to turn off the lights and bathe by candle, fine. But that may not be to everyone's taste, so make sure that the existing lights are strong enough to light the room properly.

Mirrors are often a clever way of both making a small room look bigger and enhancing the available light. Rather than having a tiny mirror over the basin, perhaps it would benefit the room to replace it with something bigger.

A lot of plants thrive in the humid atmosphere of a bathroom. Using a healthy, shiny-leaved one is a very effective way of making a dramatic statement. However, keeping several old ferns with browning leaves is not. If they don't cut it, get rid of them and buy something new.

Other stylish and economical finishing touches include: towels, which should look luxurious, neatly folded and matching; bathmat — get rid of that miserable damp rag that's seen too many wet feet and buy a new one as a present to yourself; and toilet paper — look generous with it and make sure it's not tucked away behind the lavatory where it can't be seen or reached. And finally — particularly to all you men — put down the lavatory seat!

DIAGNOSIS
& cures

The immediate problem with this bathroom was that it was far too dark. Perhaps planned as intimate and innovative, it just looked dated, gloomy and cramped. The dark red paint and stained wood ceiling did the room no favours. Worst of all, there were various unfinished DIY jobs staring any potential buyer in the face. The skirting and boxing round the pipes behind the toilet were left unpainted, while the tiles behind the basin had never found their way out of the pack and the toilet roll holder was inexplicably hung on the vertical. Bathroom products littered most of the surfaces, making the room look untidy and uncared for. When you're selling your house, it's important that the bathroom looks as light, bright and clean as possible.

Potential buyers will be put off if they think that they will have to invest in new fittings.

lighten up

The room had a good-sized window but any natural light was absorbed by the dark walls and ceiling. The solution was to paint the ceiling white and the walls a creamy yellow, which immediately made the room look larger and lighter. The white tiles were put up behind the sink and the pipe box and skirting were painted to tie in with the rest of the room. To complete the look, we bought a pale split-cane blind which gave some emphasis to the window without stopping the flood of sunlight into the room.

reduce

Everything on the edge of the bath and on top of the cabinet had to be put away so that only the barest minimum of personal items was on display. This is always the perfect moment to have a good throw-out. You probably don't need half the stuff you've got there and you certainly won't want to take it with you when you move. A buyer isn't interested in your choice of toothpaste and shampoo. Everything in this bathroom was reduced until it could happily fit into the cabinet with the doors firmly closed.

accessorise

Once the room was repainted and uncluttered, it was time to add some essential finishing touches. As our chosen keynote was blue, I found an appropriately coloured small picture to hang on the wall and a neat blue drawstring bag to hold extra soap. Buy some bars of scented soap and, if necessary, don't use them but bring them out when you've got viewers coming round. A fragrant pot-pourri was put on the cistern with a scented candle beside the toilet to ensure the room smelled as good as it now looked.

prescription STORAGE

Storage is a buzzword in contemporary design. It's true that you can't have enough storage space in a house. And it's one of the things that your potential buyers will definitely be on the lookout for. You may be happy living in a relaxed family home with things piled up on every surface, but they may be of a more minimalist bent and will want to be assured that their belongings will have their place. If you leave everything out, it gives the impression that the house is too small and doesn't have enough space to put it. You can rectify this easily by the addition of some simple storage ideas. Obviously this is not the moment to build fitted cupboards but you'll find inexpensive storage systems in your local department store or DIY shop, not to mention the specialist shops that have sprung up recently. CD and video collections should be found a home off the floor. Books should be thinned out and neatly shelved. In one house I staged, we used a third bedroom specifically as a dressing room where all the jumble from the master bedroom was neatly sorted and stored. You will be able to lay your hands on all shapes and sizes of boxes to hold photos, papers and other essential bits and pieces. Canvas wardrobes, fabric shoe holders, wine racks, mobile kitchen units are only a few of the ideas that await you. If your budget won't allow the investment, then use your attic, below-stairs space and, if the worst really comes to the worst, the boot of your car!

Alcoves on either side of the chimney breast are an ideal place for shelves.
Stuff children's toys into large plastic boxes.
Self-assembly drawers will slip neatly under a bed.
Open shelves in a kitchen are great for storage and don't make the room look smaller.
Glass shelves work brilliantly in a bathroom and even across windows sometimes.
Shelves don't have to be used for books. Ornaments can look good, too.
Make sure all cupboard doors shut properly so they don't look as if they're literally stuffed to bursting.

SELL IT!

It's essential that every room should have a clear function. You must make it clear to your buyer exactly what every room is for. Play up the existence of a dining room by clearing away all the children's homework and games. A third bedroom could be a bedroom, a study or a dressing room, but not all three at once. Organise some storage systems so that the principal function of the room they're in remains clearly defined. Furnish an empty room, giving it a *raison d'être*. If you don't want to invest in furniture before your move, ask an obliging friend if you can borrow a couple of key pieces.

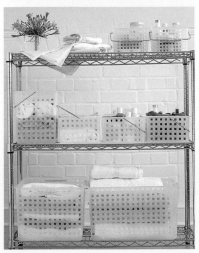

SOURCES

Left, top to bottom: These boxes could be used to hide away almost anything ★ Shoes can be a nightmare to keep tidy. A handy shoe rack makes all the difference ★ All sorts of things, from clothes to toiletries, can be neatly stored in mesh boxes on a shelving system ★ **Above:** A simple racking system can help tidy up a bathroom or kitchen ★ **Far left:** Better to hang clothes up than leave them slung over the bedroom furniture.

The Holding Company

Burlington House
184 New Kings Road
London SW6 4NF
Tel: 020 7610 9160
www.theholdingcompany.co.uk

Habitat UK Ltd

196 Tottenham Court Road
London W1P 9LD
Tel: 020 7255 2545
Website: www.habitat.co.uk

Ikea Ltd

London tel: 020 8208 5600
Croydon tel:020 8208 5601
Leeds tel:01924 423296
Thurrock tel: 01708 860868
Website: www.ikea.com

Laura Ashley

Home Customer Services
PO Box 19
Newtown
Powys SY16 1DZ
Tel: 0990 622116

Ocean Home Shopping

Freepost Lon 811
London SW8 4BR
Tel: 0800 132985

"It was as if the house was caught between two parallel universes and couldn't escape"

case STUDY

Sittingbourne is a town popular with families and commuters. It has good local facilities and with the Kent property market flourishing, it was hard for Debbie and Chris Jones to understand why their home had been on the market for six months. They were particularly anxious to sell because, after eighteen years of marriage, four children and a dog, they were getting divorced.

After looking round the house I identified the main problem. Chris and Debbie's very different tastes were reflected everywhere. I had to go one way or the other if it was going to sell. I opted to go with Debbie's taste which was light and bright. I felt it was more calculated to appeal to today's buyer than the darker, more traditional features that marked Chris's taste.

The greatest bone of contention was the enormous fireplace dominating the sitting room which Chris had built when they moved in. He felt strongly that it was in keeping with the tone of the house. I felt that it was too overbearing and, combined with decorative horse brasses, came from another decade. So against his wishes, we

"The fireplace was laid to rest in a hardboard casket and, using two coats of Marmorino plaster and a colour wash to give a contemporary feel, it was resurrected as Italian marble"

boxed it in. Because the living room was so dark, we also replaced the deep red carpet with a paler, more neutral colour. With a final rearrangement of the furniture so that the sitting and dining areas were clearly defined, plus the addition of some toning cushions to break up the solid red of the sofas, the room was transformed.

I insisted all the ceilings in the house were painted white so that they seemed higher and the rooms seemed lighter. The kitchen was bland and rather old-fashioned, but it was brought to life with a new coat of green paint on the walls and by resurrecting some of Debbie's green, yellow and blue china for effect. At the other end of the room we played up the breakfast bar, making a feature of it.

Upstairs the master bedroom (which had become Chris's) was again "of an era". The wallpaper was coming off the walls to prove it! Although downstairs was vastly improved, it was still important to present the whole house in the best possible light. So we stripped the walls, then painted them a neutral colour with some punch — a pale terracotta. Then I simply accented the room with blue duvet, curtains and table tops.

Although Debbie was convinced, Chris still had his reservations about the treatment, saying it was "chaotic" and "tortuous". Nonetheless, within 30 days, they were happily sitting on three offers at the asking price.

prescription FLOORING

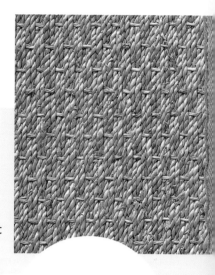

The choice and condition of your floor coverings says a lot about you to the buyer. Make sure it's all good by looking at the carpet and asking yourself if something else wouldn't look better. Take the period of your house into consideration. A hip rubber floor will look quite wrong in a Georgian town house, while wall-to-wall carpet may look out of place in the most modern house. There's a huge range of carpets and other materials to choose from, so before you replace, think about what the room is used for. Also remember that, ideally, you're not going to live with it forever, so don't go for the bright red or sunshine yellow that you love. Choose the plain, the neutral, the understated. These won't offend a buyer's eye and have the advantage of apparently enlarging the floor space too. Seagrass matting can be a practical alternative, if a little unfriendly to bare feet and crawling babies. Should the idea of buying carpet be too daunting, look at the floorboards beneath. Bare varnished boards often look great with a couple of rugs thrown on them. Rugs are a good way of bringing together the colour scheme in a room, too. In the kitchen or bathroom, the floors should clean up thoroughly or you should replace the covering. Whatever you use should be waterproof and hard-wearing. Again, there's a huge range of choice, but err on the side of the neutrals. The flooring should always recede into the background, letting your furnishings speak for themselves.

- Replace kitchen and bathroom carpet with something hard-wearing and easy to clean – perhaps tiles (vinyl or ceramic), lino or wood.
- Choose neutral colours so the carpet fades into the background.
- Remember what the room is being used for when you choose the floor covering.
- You will need a hard-wearing carpet for the hall and stairway.
- A dark staircase and hall can often be dramatically improved by a lighter neutral shade of carpet.
- Stain and varnish floorboards or paint them with specialist hard-wearing paint.

SELL IT!

Your carpet can play a big role in a successful house sale. A carpet that is dark or heavily patterned dominates a room and makes it seem smaller. A smelly, damp carpet is a real bathroom turn-off. Dining rooms with food trodden into the floor are out. The same goes if it is old, worn or just dirty. A new carpet may seem an unnecessary expense, but it will lift the appearance of the room and your buyers won't be imagining the extra cost of replacing it themselves. Make it easy for them to like your house.

SOURCES

Ammonite Flooring
22 Hayes Street
Hayes
Kent B12 7LD
Tel: 020 8462 4671

Amtico Co Ltd
Kingfield Road
Coventry CV6 5AA
Tel: 0800 667766

Carpet Warehouse
Unit 2
Donisthorpe Street
Hunslet Road
Leeds LS10 1JN
Tel: 0113 243 1117

**Ceramic Prints Ltd
(floor tiles)**
George Street
Armitage Road Industrial Estate
Brighouse
West Yorkshire HD6 1PU
Tel: 01484 712522
www.ceramic\print.com

Crucial Trading
PO Box 11
Duke Place
Kidderminster
Worcestershire DY10 2JR
Tel: 01562 825656
www.crucial-trading.com

Clockwise, left to right: Coir matting comes in different weaves which provide interest in an otherwise neutral floor covering. It is hard-wearing and ideal for any room except kitchen and bathroom ★ A floating hardwood floor provides a clean and modern finish for all rooms ★ Amtico floor tiles offer an excellent, hard-wearing, easy-to-clean finish ★ A combination of Amtico and hardwood offers a floor treatment with a difference. ★ **Far left**: Linoleum has come a long way since the 1950s.

the CURE

mess

If it looks like a tip, your bathroom won't help you sell your house. There's no need to have all that junk on the floor, or on the cistern. This bathroom gave the impression that it was dirty and uncared-for.

paint it

All it took was a lick of lilac paint for this dreary bathroom to be transformed into somewhere funky and contemporary. The look was completed with the clean white tiles that ran along the walls by the basin and toilet.

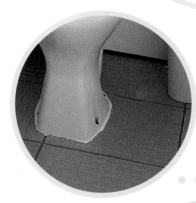

flooring

That ghastly green bathmat hit the dustbin, while the tired old flooring was replaced with some stylish grey tiles which blend in with the new colour scheme and complete a much more modern look.

shelving

Rather than an ugly bathroom cabinet, these owners opted for a couple of glass shelves which hardly intrude on the room and provide storage for a <u>select</u> number of things.

before

"Inexpensive bedding plants will invigorate the dreariest plot"

Chapter Seven
GARDENS

A garden can be a huge asset when selling a house. It should be seen as another room, an extension of the indoors, which can be enjoyed just as much. Your buyers will relish the idea of being able to sit outside in the summer enjoying the fruits of your labours and adding some of their own. But it's the place that's all too easy to overlook, particularly if it has been taken over by pets or children. When did you last look at the state they've left it in? Now's the time to do just that.

You needn't remove all signs of the children's existence, but you should lose all signs of untidiness. If you've got too many plastic bikes and outdoor playthings, it might be wise to invest in a small shed where they can be hidden away. However, that muddy football pitch is much more difficult to hide so, depending on the time of year, you could returf and ban all games till further notice! If your dog has been using the garden as his exercise run and toilet then it may be another case for returfing and taking him to the local park for the next few weeks. And as for the kennel? Move it to as discreet a position as possible. Reminders of your pet here are as unlikely to do anything for the sale of your house as they would inside. Take down the washing line and make sure that any rubbish which is long overdue for the dump is finally taken there.

Now for the garden itself. Repair any broken walls or fencing. If you're fortunate enough not to have had to returf, then mow your lawn and trim the edge. A proprietary weedkiller should clear up the gaps between the patio flagstones and any garden path.

If you have an old fruit tree, it might look more charming if it were pruned (again, depending on the time of year) and you should certainly remove any windfalls and fallen leaves in the autumn. As for the flowerbeds, a quick trip to a garden centre (no matter what season) will provide you with some inexpensive bedding plants which will invigorate the dreariest plot for at least as long as it takes to sell it.

Another way of adding colour to a garden is to paint one of the walls a cheerful colour and add some hanging baskets. The oldest trick in the book is to put a mirror on a blank wall which will make the garden seem much bigger. This can work wonders with a small patio garden, particularly when the edges of the mirror are hidden by plants.

You should go through your pot plants thoroughly, replacing any dead ones or removing the pot altogether.

Garden or patio furniture is easy to find at your local garden centre, nearby department store or DIY centre. The upside is that you can, of course, take it with you when you move. A judiciously placed table and a couple of chairs will always draw people into the garden on a sunny day. They will be able to imagine themselves entertaining friends or dining "al fresco". For a real finishing touch, how about a fountain or water feature? It creates the feeling of serenity everyone wants from their outdoor "sanctuary".

jumble

The same principles apply to outside space as to indoor. Every area should be clearly defined so that any potential buyer can immediately identify what it's used for. You must try to present each space, including the garden, in the most inviting way possible. Having an old junk yard out at the back will not do you any favours at all. As ever, any unnecessary clutter must be cleared away. This roof terrace looked unloved and ignored. The owners had dumped rusty bicycle frames, dead plants and anything else they didn't want out there. Once this mess was removed, things began to improve.

DIAGNOSIS
& cures

When selling your house, you should make the most of every asset you have. If it's a good property, you should make it look a great property. In this case, I was horrified to find that the roof terrace had been completely overlooked. Every space in a house must be maximised and outdoor space is a big plus, particularly for a town house. There was room here to create another area for the owners to sit – and even eat – outside. It only needed a few touches to put things right.

garden furniture

A good set of garden table and chairs immediately gives purpose to an outside space. There are so many different styles to choose from these days that you need to think carefully about the overall look you want to achieve before buying. The wooden furniture we chose for this terrace has a simple rustic appeal which suits the space it inhabits. Go to your local garden centre or nearby large department store to investigate the range of furniture available.

privacy

On the whole, people prefer not to be overlooked when they're out enjoying themselves in the garden. A buyer will love any impression of somewhere quiet and relatively secluded. One way of doing this cheaply is to put up some trellising above your garden/roof-terrace wall and grow climbers in pots which will eventually cover it and provide a protective screen. This also has the added advantage of hiding an unattractive view. It may not seem a quick solution, but you'll be surprised at the speed with which a solanum or clematis can grow.

children and pets

Taking pride of place next to the barbecue was an unused children's sandpit. One of my absolute rules is that evidence of children should be removed wherever possible. Not, of course, that there's anything wrong with them really. It's just that the amount of coloured plastic of so many different shapes and sizes which comes with them can be very distracting to buyers and put them off the business of evaluating your home as somewhere they might be able to live. The same goes for pets, too. Nobody will want to live with the damage your beloved Fido has wreaked on what might otherwise be a strong selling point for your house.

DIAGNOSIS
& cures

This yard was suffering from terrible neglect. There was a barbecue out there, but it was hardly a space where anyone would want to spend much time, least of all relaxing with a beer and a spare rib! The only thing to look at was the sparsely planted flower bed and a few empty plant pots. Not an attractive sight. The paintwork was looking very tired, too. I had to find a way to transform this yard into somewhere alive and welcoming.

colour

It's always possible to jazz up a dead space by adding colour. In this case we concentrated on the green of the plants and any other colour would come from their flowers. However, had the budget allowed, we could have been a little more experimental, painting the door a strong colour and maybe even one of the walls as well, to add interest.

plants

Dead plants and even just uncared-for plants add nothing whatsoever to the appearance of a garden. Empty flowerpots look forlorn and depressing. Go down to your local garden centre and ask their advice about the sort of plants that would grow happily in your patch. Then, suitably armed, return home, throw away the unhealthy specimens and design a simple planting plan. In this garden we chose plants in a range of heights and foliage so we could create something consistently interesting to look at.

> "As the front door opened, it hit a small table standing right behind it. The room was dominated by a long sofa, a favourite place for Ben to sit between his owners of an evening. The carpet was pretty dingy and there was a slight but distinct smell of dog"

case STUDY

Rachel, Dean and their dog Ben were living in a small end-of-terrace Victorian cottage. They were keen to sell before their baby was due to be born four months later. Headcorn is a small Kentish village within London's commuter belt where there is normally a waiting list for properties. This one had been for sale for ten months. Rachel and Dean were well aware that potential buyers were concerned the place was too small, so they had done some repainting and tidying up. Nonetheless, Ben's presence was still strongly felt, with his photo in pole position over the cluttered mantelpiece (it was almost the first thing you noticed on walking in). The kitchen was cramped, crowded and not in keeping with the period feel of the cottage. Upstairs in the main bedroom, the furniture was arranged so that the window was blocked by the bed and the storage units took up too much space. Worst of all though, was the dog's bed ...

Meanwhile, outside, the large garden was a tip. Potentially a strong selling point, the patio was claimed by an old armchair which was waiting for a trip to the dump.

The obvious problem was lack of space — and more lack of space. What I had to do was find a way to maximise the space there was and create the illusion of there being more. One way of doing this is to use mirrors to give more dimension to the rooms. Otherwise, I had to insist that, because not everyone's a dog lover, Ben's influence had to go. They weren't happy. But my job wasn't to make them happy, it was to sell their house. Since the living room was the first thing seen by anyone coming into the house, I decided Rachel and Dean should replace the carpet and the sofa, even though they were a gift from their Uncle Dave. With seagrass matting on the floor and the walls painted buttermilk instead of pink, things were starting to look better. We bought a two-seater sofa which toned with the curtains and cushions and was the right size to allow the fireplace to become the focal point of the room. It's important to get rid of too many personal influences in a room — too much personality and your prospective buyer will end

up making judgements about you and not your house — so the picture of Ben had to go, despite protests, and was replaced by a mirror which immediately made the room feel bigger. Out went the small table behind the front door and in came some wire and wicker furniture, more strategically placed. Fortunately there was a shed in the garden which we could use for all temporarily unwanted clutter.

The trick with the kitchen was to make the most of the extremely limited area. We extended the seagrass flooring to run from the living room into the kitchen to give the impression of a continuing space. Another mirror was fitted into a semicircular brick arch at the end of the counter, making it apparently stretch to infinity. I found some antiquey, cottagey handles for the units which softened the general effect and fitted with the period feel of the house. A major difference was made to the bedroom by simply moving the furniture around. The wardrobe and chest of drawers fitted neatly into the spare room, making a dressing room. Already the room felt more spacious and relaxed. By moving the bed, we unblocked the window, and by adding a navy valance and curtains we eliminated conflicting patterns. Ben's basket was the last to go and with it, that distinctive smell. I relented enough to let Rachel and

Dean hang his photo among a montage of framed pictures instead.

Lastly, the garden. When I arrived it looked like the town dump, so I got rid of anything that wasn't usable or inviting. The armchair finally made way for a smart white garden table and chairs. It only took a few simple bedding plants to transform the outdoor space into another functional living space.

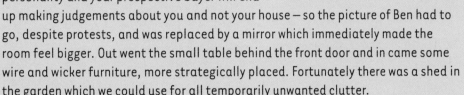

"It's important to get rid of too many personal influences in a room – too much personality and your prospective buyers will end up making judgements about you and not your house"

the
CURE

design

This small garden was too busy. Everything jostled for attention. What it needed was a strong but simple design which would pull it into one coherent look, doing justice to, and maximising, the space available.

decking

An impressive-looking solution to a hideous patio, or even a strip of grass used for football practice, is decking. Surprisingly inexpensive, it can be quick and easy to put down with immediate and stylish results.

trellising

A stretch of trellising doesn't have to be throttled by climbing plants to be effective. Here, it provided additional height to the wall, further defining the boundary but without interrupting the light falling on the garden.

simplicity

The keynote of the new garden was simplicity. Too many things in a small space make it look claustrophobic. The garden bench and table add a note of elegant sophistication which is emphasised by the sparing choice of pot plants.

before

the CURE

rubbish

Of course gardens all look much better when the dead leaves and general garden debris are removed. But make sure the rubbish bin and tools are removed too, otherwise the final impression is spoilt.

focus

This garden had everything beautifully arranged along the edges. What it lacked was a focal point, which was provided by creating an area for relaxing and/or entertaining. The café-style table and chairs tied in well to the feel of this town garden.

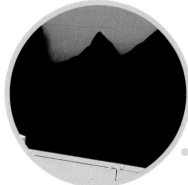

comfort

Sitting outside doesn't have to be an ordeal. The dead space along one part of the fencing provided a sheltered arbour where large, squashy cushions begged to be sat on, in a spot where even the most jaded of town dwellers would relax.

under foot

Flagstones can begin to look green and slippery if they're not religiously cared for. For a completely different, more informal look, white gravel was poured over them. It was an inexpensive treatment which can easily be changed but which gives new life and light to the garden.

before

after

GENERAL

Aero
96 Westbourne Road
London W2 5RT
Tel: 020 7221 1950

B & Q
Portswood House
1 Hampshire Corporate Park
Chandlers Ford
Hampshire SO53 3YX
Head office tel: 023 8025 6256
Store location tel: 023 8466 4166
Website: www.dfy.com

The Building Centre
26 Store Street
London WC1 7BT
Tel: 020 7692 4040

Habitat UK Ltd
(picture above)
196 Tottenham Court Road
London W1P 9LD
Tel: 020 7255 2545
Website: www.habitat.co.uk

Homebase
Beddington House, Railway Approach
Wallington
Surrey SM6 0HB
Tel: 020 8784 7200
Website: www.homebase.co.uk

Ikea Ltd
2 Drury Way
North Circular Road
London NW10 0JO
Customer Service tel: 020 8208 5600
Website: www.ikea.com

John Lewis
Oxford Street
London W1A 1EX
Tel: 020 7629 7711
Website: www.johnlewispartnership.co.uk

Laura Ashley
Home Customer Services PO Box 19
Newtown
Powys SY16 1DZ
Tel: 0990 622116

Ocean Home Shopping
Freepost Lon 811
London SW8 4BR
Tel: 0870 848 4840

The Pier
200 Tottenham Court Road
London W1P 0AD
Tel: 020 7637 7001

Wickes (head office)
120-138 Station Road
Harrow
Middlesex HA1 2QB
Customer Enquiries tel: 0500 300328

ACCESSORIES

David Cook Pottery
Spring Cottage
Church Street
Upwey
Weymouth
Dorset DT3 5QE
Tel: 01305 812665

Elephant
230 Tottenham Court Road
London W1P 9AE
Tel: 020 7637 7930

The Factory Shop
The Foreman Centre
High Street
Headcorn
Kent TN27 9NE
Tel: 01622 891651

Picture Warehouse
Abbey Road Motor Centre
Belsize Road
London NW6 4AB
Tel: 020 7328 6915

Spoils Kitchen Reject Shop
Bath Street
Ipswich
Suffolk IP2 8SD
Tel: 01473 603666

Take Cover (linen, curtains)
142 Church Street
Edgware
London NW8 8EX
Tel: 020 7258 1171

Texstyle World
Store info tel: 08452 727374

ARCHITECTURAL IRONMONGERY
Danico Brass Ltd

31-35 Winchester Road
London NW3 3NR
Tel: 020 7483 4477
e-mail: dannico@compuserve.com

BATHROOMS
Aqualisa Products Ltd

The Flyer's Way
Westerham
Kent TN16 1DE
Tel: 01959 560020
Website: www.aqualisa.co.uk

Eastbrook Co.

Eastbrook Road
Gloucester GL4 3DB
Tel: 01452 317800

Imperial Towel Rails

Jupiter House
Orbital Way
Cannock
Staffs WS11 3XW
Tel: 01543 571615

BLINDS
Tidmarsh

32 Hyde Way
Welwyn Garden City
Herts AL7 3AW
Tel: 01707 886226
Website: www.bbsa\uk.com

DOORS
'Er in Doors

35 Beech Road
St Albans
Herts
Tel: 01727 811921

DOORS & WINDOWS
Marshall Tufflex Ltd

Ponswood
Hastings TN34 1YJ
Tel: 01424 427691

FIREPLACES
Marble Hill Fireplaces

(picture above)
70-72 Richmond Road
Twickenham
Middx TW1 3BE
Tel: 020 8892 1488
Website: www.marblehill.co.uk

FLOORING
Ammonite Flooring

22 Hayes Street
Hayes
Kent B12 7LD
Tel: 020 8462 4671

Amtico Co Ltd

Kingfield Road
Coventry CV6 5AA
Tel: 0800 667766

Carpet Warehouse

Unit 2 Donisthorpe Street, Hunslet Road
Leeds LS10 1JN
Tel: 0113 243 1117

Crucial Trading

PO Box 11

Duke Place

Kidderminster

Worcestershire

DY10 2JR

Tel: 01562 825656

Website: www.crucial-trading.com

Kingsmead Carpets

Caponacre Industrial Estate

Cumnock

Ayrshire KA18 1SH

Tel: 01290 421 511

Knutsford Floor Coverings (lino)

15 Princess Street

Knutsford

WA16 6BY

Tel: 01565 632542

Natural Flooring Direct

47 Webbs Road

London SW11 6BR

Tel: 0800 454721

e-mail: nfd@eidonet.com

KITCHENS
Harvey Jones Ltd

57 New Kings Road

London SW6 4SE

Tel: 0800 9172340

The Magnet Co.

Royd Ings Road

Keighley

Yorks BD21 4BY

Tel: 01535 661133

Rhode Design

137-139 Essex Road

London N1 2NR

Tel: 020 7354 9933

LIGHTING
Christopher Wray

591-593 Kings Road

London SW6 2YW

Catalogue tel: 020 7384 2888

Enquiries tel: 020 7736 8434

Website: www.christopherwray.com

PAINTS/WALL-COVERINGS
Crown Decorative Products Ltd

Crown House

Hollins Road

Darwen, Lancashire BB3 0BG

Tel: 01254 704951

Dulux Paints

ICI Paint

Wexham Road

Slough

Berks SL2 5DS

Tel: 01753 550000

Advice tel line:

Retail: 01753 556998

Trade: 01753 559991

Website: www.dulux.co.uk

International Tile Paints

Plascon International Ltd

Brewery House

High Street

Twyford

Winchester SO21 1RG

Enquiries tel: 01962 711503

Website: www.plascon.co.uk

Paint Magic

48 Golborne Road

London W10 5PR

Tel: 020 8960 9910

Website: www.paint.magic.com

RADIATORS
Bisque London Showroom

244 Belsize Road

London NW6 8TU

Tel: 020 7586 9749

Nationwide tel: 01225 469 244

e-mail: sfs.pr@easynet.co.uk

Caradon Plumbing Ltd

Lawton Road

Alsager

Stoke-on-Trent ST7 2DF

Tel: 0870 840100

Classic Radiator Covers Co

Unit 2 and 5 Mountain Ash Industrial Estate

Mountain Ash

Mid Glamorgan CF45 4EY

For brochure, tel: 01443 477824

Clyde Combustions Ltd

Cox Lane

Chessington

Surrey KT9 1SL

Tel: 020 8391 2020

Potterton Myson Ltd
Eastern Avenue
Team Valley Trading Estate
Gateshead
Tyne & Wear NE11 0PG
Tel: 0191 491 4466
Website: www.myson.co.uk

The Radiator Cover Co.
For brochure, tel: 0800 328 5074

Redring Electric Ltd
Morley Way
Peterborough PE2 9JJ
Tel: 01733 456789
Website: www.redring.com

Walney
Stanton Square
Stanton Way
London SE26 5AB
Tel: 020 8659 3430
email info@pmp-walney.co.uk
Website: www.pmp.walney.co.uk

Zehnder
Invincible Road
Farnborough
Hants GU14 7QU
Tel: 01252 515151
Telex: 858093

STORAGE
The Holding Company
(picture at left)
Burlington House
184 New Kings Road
London SW6 4NF
Tel: 020 7610 9160
Website: www.the holding company.co.uk

TILES
Ceramic Prints Ltd
George Street
Armitage Road Industrial Estate
Brighouse
West Yorkshire HD6 1PU
Tel: 01484 712522
Website: www.ceramic\print.com

Elon
For brochure, tel: 020 8932 6132

Pilkington's Tiles Ltd
PO Box 4
Clifton Junction
Manchester M27 8LP
Tel: 0161 727 1000

Worlds End Tiles
(picture above)
Silverthorne Road
Battersea
London SW8 3HE
Tel: 020 7819 2100
Website: www.worldsendtiles.co.uk

photographs